Cultivating Professional Friendships in Early Childhood Education

Cultivating Professional Friendships

in Early Childhood Education

Diane Kashin

Redleaf Press®
www.redleafpress.org
800-423-8309

Published by Redleaf Press
10 Yorkton Court
St. Paul, MN 55117
www.redleafpress.org

First edition 2023
Cover design by Becky Daum
Cover illustration by melita/stock.adobe.com
Interior design by Louise OFarrell
Typeset in Freight Text Pro
Printed in the United States of America

Library of Congress Cataloging-in-Publication Data
Names: Kashin, Diane, author.
Title: Cultivating professional friendships in early childhood education / by Diane Kashin.
Description: First edition. | St. Paul, MN : Redleaf Press, [2024] | Includes bibliographical references. | Summary: "Using a parallel process that makes connections to children's friendships, author Diane Kashin draws on a wealth of research and a lifetime of professional friendships to invite readers to muse with her on what it means to be a friend, how to make friends and keep friends, and what happens when friendships end"— Provided by publisher.
Identifiers: LCCN 2023019534 (print) | LCCN 2023019535 (ebook) | ISBN 9781605547961 (paperback) | ISBN 9781605547978 (ebook)
Subjects: LCSH: Early childhood teachers—Professional relationships. | Early childhood education—Social aspects. | Professional learning communities. | Mentoring in education. | Friendship in children.
Classification: LCC LB1775.6 .K37 2024 (print) | LCC LB1775.6 (ebook) | DDC 372.21--dc23/eng/20230510
LC record available at https://lccn.loc.gov/2023019534
LC ebook record available at https://lccn.loc.gov/2023019535

Printed on acid-free paper U24-04

Dedicated to my friends who are like family
and my family who are like friends

Contents

Acknowledgments xi

Introduction ▧ **Reflecting on Professional Friendships** 1

Professional and Critical Friends 2

Learning from Giants 4

Child and Adult Friendships Compared 6

You Deserve a Professional Friend! 8

Love and Layers 10

The Seasons of Friendship 12

Beginning with Gratitude 14

Chapter One ▧ **Forming Friendships: The Birth of Peer-to-Peer Relationships** 17

Hello, Friend! 17

The Act of Reflection 18

Spheres of Friendships 21

Professional Interests 22

The Power of Professional Friends 24

Big Ideas of Professional Friendships: Identity 26

From a Basis of Trust 29

Thank You for Being a Friend 33

Four Questions for My Friend: Cindy 34

Chapter Two ▧ **Forging Friendships: Engaging the Heart** 37

Hello, Friend! 37

Friendships Take Time and Effort 40

Listening to Our Emotions 41
Listening to Our Friends 44
The Languages of Professional Friendships 46
Professional Friendship and Self-Doubt 49
Professional Friends Empower 51
Big Ideas of Professional Friendships: Values 54
Thank You for Being a Friend 55
Four Questions for My Friend: Rosalba 57

Chapter Three ▧ **Forging Friendships: Reaching the Spirit** 61
Hello, Friend! 61
Parallels between Children and Adults 63
Coming to the Edge of the Circle 65
Applying the Seasonal Pedagogy to Play 68
Power, Language, and Relationships 71
Spiritual Perspectives 72
What, Then What, So What, Now What? 74
Big Ideas of Professional Friendships: Reciprocity 75
Names and Knowing Each Other 76
Invitations from Mother Earth 79
Thank You for Being a Friend 81
Four Questions for My Friend: Hopi 81

Chapter Four ▧ **Forging Friendships: Activating the Mind** 83
Hello, Friend! 83
True and Lasting Friendships 84
When Friendships End 85
Disagreements as Opportunities 88
Time for New Friendships 91
Somersaulting with Friends 92
Thinking in a Circle 94
The Healing Value of Play 96

Filling Your Empty Cup 97
Playing to Empower 99
Big Ideas of Professional Friendships: Play 100
Playing Tea Party 101
Thank You for Being a Friend 102
Four Questions for My Friend: Suzanne 103

Chapter Five ▧ **Constructing Friendships: Making Connections** 107
Hello, Friend! 107
Perspective Taking Involves Trust 110
Agency in Professional Learning 112
Be the Power 114
The Yin and Yang Perspective 114
Big Ideas of Professional Friendships: Shared Interests 116
Sharing Feedback 118
Slowing Down 120
Thank You for Being a Friend 122
Four Questions for My Friend: Miriam 124

Chapter Six ▧ **Circles of Friends: Communities of Support** 127
Hello, Friend! 127
Building Friendships to Last a Lifetime 128
Cultivating Cultures of Friendship 129
Making Friendship Visible 133
Calling a Circle of Friends 136
Find the Power 140
Big Ideas of Professional Friendships: Legacy and Giving Back 142
Thank You for Being a Friend 144
Four Questions for My Circle of Friends 146

References 149

Acknowledgments

I have always believed that early childhood educators are the salt of the earth, a phrase that refers to groups of people who have great worth to society. It is for those who work with children day in and day out that I wrote this book. I want to acknowledge and value your work by sharing these pages of support, encouragement, challenge, and provocation on the hopefully relatable topic of professional friendships. The friends we work with can offer so much to our practice and our lives.

I was moved to write this book because of a friendship that sadly ended. The process of writing has been cathartic, and I am left with only feelings of love and respect for all the friends who have been a part of my long career in early childhood education. Each and every one has been a gift that I acknowledge and appreciate.

In particular, my friend Miriam Beloglovsky's encouragement and support challenged me to think of the topic for this book. I want to acknowledge and thank Miriam for this "aha" moment that has changed my life. It led me to the best editor an author could have. My final acknowledgment is for Melissa York, whose kind and insightful suggestions have scaffolded my thinking and my writing.

Paola and Sheila Reunited

Photo Credit: Deb Bumbstead

Introduction

Reflecting on Professional Friendships

It is through others that we
develop into ourselves. ~ Lev Vygotsky

When Sheila met Paola, she had just moved to a new town to work at a recently opened university child care center. Paola helped train Sheila, and their friendship grew. Together they were part of a tight-knit group of young early childhood educators, and they celebrated many milestones together while supporting each other through difficult and challenging times. Years later, Sheila moved, and Paola took on a new role. Eventually, they connected through social media, but a chance meeting in the summer of 2022 brought an emotional reunion. They had shared so many memories and experiences together, and now they had so much to catch up on in a short amount of time. Sheila and Paola described the reunion as like coming home. The power of professional friendships cannot be underestimated, especially for early childhood educators. Friendships forged in work environments can lead to professional growth as well as a lifetime of support, encouragement, and love.

Do you have an early-career friendship that has endured? The friends that educators make at the beginning of their careers can have a lifelong impact. According to data collected in a Gallup poll, when employees affirm that they have a best friend at work, they have higher job satisfaction and less stress. Conversely, the absence of workplace friends results in loneliness (Goldberg 2022). Our professional friends are a salve for feelings of isolation.

This book is about cultivating professional friendships in early childhood education. To *cultivate* is to intentionally work on making something stronger. Friendships need time and attention to be forged into strong relationships that hold up over the years. A *friendship* describes the state of being friends. A friendship is a relationship of mutual affection between two people. The relationship between colleagues can grow so that it offers both parties support. Some of us even see these friends from work more often than friends from other friendship spheres. We rely on our professional friends for day-to-day cooperation and collaboration. We turn to our professional friends because they understand the context of our working lives. We can learn from our professional friends in ways that can be just as effective as reading a professional book or attending a workshop. With intention, these relationships can be sources of sustenance for our professional practices.

When we consider our work contexts as ecosystems, communities of living things interacting with one another, we can see the potential of a layered approach. Early childhood educators can cultivate a culture of friendship across all layers of the early childhood education ecosystem, nurturing the growth of friendships for children, with families, and with one another.

Professional and Critical Friends

The concept of professional friends is influenced by research on critical friendships. Educational consultants Arthur L. Costa and Bena Kallick introduced the theory of critical friendship in 1993. A critical friendship is a complex relationship between two colleagues. A critical friend asks provocative questions and provides different lenses to view and examine practices. A critical friend offers critiques while avoiding criticism. A critique requires a constructive and impersonal description of what is being observed in a manner that is specific and informed, while criticism is about making judgments and finding faults. There can be a fine line between the two, but when that line is crossed and criticism is offered, it can hurt the other person and be misinterpreted.

Critical friendship has been examined in many educational contexts (Baskerville and Goldblatt 2009), but few research articles have been written from the perspective of early childhood education. This book suggests that while a critical friend is valuable because they understand your professional context and goals, early childhood educators need friends who go beyond this to champion and challenge thinking, being, and practice within layers of love and kindness. Early childhood educators understand that our foundation is love and kindness. My use of the term *professional friends* rather than *critical friends* is intentional in this book. Critique is a worthy goal but often crosses the line into criticism. We need relationships that focus more on encouragement and support and less on critique or criticism. Focusing on love rather than the need to offer a detached descriptive review is a kind gift we can offer our friends.

This book is your invitation to see your professional friendships as crucial to your development without feeling a need to critique. Friendships across the layers of the early childhood education ecosystem reflect states of enduring affection, esteem, and trust within dyadic relationships, between two people bonded by love. Professional friends have a great affection for each other, and they work from a place of kindness to create a culture based on love.

Professional friendships are vital to surviving and thriving within the complex early childhood ecosystem and to developing our pedagogy as early childhood educators. Professional friends encourage each other to be critically reflective. When we reflect and collaborate together, it can bolster and uplift our professional learning. Can you recall an experience you had with a work friend when you engaged in a shared experience and learned together? Pause and think about professional friends you have had over the course of your career, and visualize an example. You can also think about current professional friends as well as imagine who might be a potential friend.

1. Who comes to mind?
2. What made you think of them?
3. What descriptors would you use to portray the relationship?
4. What sustained or didn't sustain the relationship?
5. What feelings has this thought exercise evoked?

Friendships live on in our lives even when the friend is no longer there. Engaging in a reflective process about past, present, and future professional friendships is an opportunity to consider your legacy, what you will pass on to the next generation of early childhood educators.

Cultivating your professional friendships requires you to consider what your friends mean to you and your practice. Friendships are complex and intense; therefore, critical reflection is necessary to make meaning of them. Think about what being a friend means. A friend is someone with whom you share affection, experiences, and values. A friend is someone you trust. The relationship is characterized by mutual respect for each other's well-being.

At the core of a friendship is care, something we know about in early childhood education! This type of friend is different from the social media definition of a friend. On social media platforms, you are in a friendship when your two accounts are linked together. Social media "friends" are not automatically real-life friends, as being a friend is more of a verb than a passive state of being. To be a friend is to act as a friend in a reciprocal fashion.

The construct of friendship implies a reciprocity of give-and-take. Friends expect that support flows both ways as the need arises for either friend. Regardless of the inconvenience or challenges they may face, a true friend can be counted on to offer help. Professional friendships flourish when there is mutual respect and mutual trust. From this basis of trust, your friend is a sounding board who supports you to be the best version of yourself.

Professional friendships form voluntarily and are characterized by interdependence. *Interdependence* is the dependence of two people on each other because each takes pleasure in the other's company. When a friendship becomes about anything else, it may be fleeting. When it becomes a duty rather than a preference, it will wane and eventually dissolve. If it doesn't terminate, the friendship can become intensely toxic. This is not what we want in our professional relationships. It is not what we want for children's friendships.

Think about your colleagues. Are they professional friends waiting to happen? Intentionally cultivating a professional relationship into a friendship will give you someone who will

- always be there for you,
- listen to you,
- be empathetic toward you,
- forgive you, if necessary, and
- love you.

To go from being a colleague to being a friend puts you in a next-level relationship. A true friend is always there for you, listening and forgiving with empathy. I want that for myself, for my friends, for you, and for all children.

Learning from Giants

Ten years ago, Lella Gandini, the North American liaison for the Reggio Emilia approach, was visiting Toronto, and I was assigned the honor of being her driver. Listening to her speak of her professional relationship with Loris Malaguzzi (1920–1994), who has influenced my philosophy, practice, and understanding of pedagogy, was unforgettable. Child psychologist and author David Elkind (2015) refers to those who have historically influenced early childhood education as "giants in the nursery." The day I spent with Gandini, I felt as though I was in the presence of a giant in early childhood education.

I deeply appreciate the work of others whose theories and ideas influence my thinking. They help me arrive at a higher level of reflection as I engage with their perspectives. When I consider the words of others, I am also developing my own capacity to be a theorist. Journalist and author Kate Murphy (2020) suggests that when we reflect on what someone has said, the thoughts and feelings of that person take up space in our hearts and minds. We make connections that activate our acquisition of knowledge. This is constructivism in action.

The theories of Swiss psychologist Jean Piaget (1896–1980) represented the dominant view of early childhood during the time I was becoming an early childhood educator, and I connected to his philosophy of constructivism. According to the theory, knowledge is acquired through active involvement with content instead of through imitation or memorization. In an early childhood context, this means a child acquires knowledge through play rather than through rote learning. This made sense to me, but something was missing. While Piaget viewed knowledge as being constructed from personal experiences, Russian psychologist Lev Vygotsky (1896–1934) maintained that personal and social experiences could not be separated. Social constructivism has come to define my work as I continue to learn within a social construct, especially from my professional friends.

Play should figure prominently among professional friends. In the *American Journal of Play*, Gandini recalls that "Malaguzzi said very clearly that nothing in the school should happen without joy" and that he would not have separated play and learning (Gandini 2011, 7). Marcia Nell, Walter Drew, and Deborah Bush (2013, 1) suggest that when "teachers engage in self-active play and personally experience its social, emotional, physical, and cognitive benefits, they develop a clearer insight into what children gain from play." These advocates for play believe that the ability to play and to remain playful is essential to children and their teachers. They reinforce what has always been a focus of my work, which is the inclusion of play in professional learning.

Which giants have influenced your work? Gandini had a close relationship to Malaguzzi and often translated his words. When I was with her, she shared a story about introducing Malaguzzi to David Hawkins (1913–2002), which led to a historic professional friendship. Hawkins was a professor and a philosopher of science, with an interest in mathematics, economics, education, and ethics. He was married to Frances Hawkins (1914–2006), an expert in early childhood education. Malaguzzi and David Hawkins shared many values, including the importance of playing with materials. Teachers, like children, need to "mess about."

With inspiration from the giants of early learning, let's take time to mess about with the big ideas of professional friendships. Through reflection and dialogue with our friends, *we* will become giants in our own right.

Child and Adult Friendships Compared

Early childhood education expert Carolyn Pope Edwards (1946–2018), another giant in the sector, wrote about children's friendships. She describes friendship as one of the good things in life that can be enjoyed at any stage of life, but in the early years, these relationships are *proto-friendships*, or first friendships. What do these proto-friendships mean to children? And how do they see these relationships as different from those with their family members? Edwards suggests that children are continually thinking about friendships as they navigate the social and moral rules of these complex relationships. Friendships are more than personalities that fit together, shared interests, and common experiences, and they deserve close attention over time as they can bring both joy and sorrow to a child. Edwards suggests that we consider these three elements of children's friendships to begin the process of understanding them:

1. Children's concepts of friendship develop over time. Some peer-to-peer friendships are immediate and activity-based. Other friendships are characterized by deep attachments to others, to both children and adults. With these proto-friendships, there is a sustained level of play and "complex reciprocities of turn-taking and kindness" (Edwards 2004, 30).
2. The tools of friendship are acquired over time. Language that helps children communicate with potential friends develops from words like *no* and *come here* to "more subtle constructions like *If I . . . will you . . .* or *I would play if . . .* " (Edwards 2004, 31). The language of internal states

gradually appears as children learn to distinguish between feeling *mad* at being left out of play and feeling *sad* to have been excluded.

3 Over time, friendships will take many forms. Children are not just working to understand a single concept of friendship; they are working out the differences between relationships with peers and relationships with their parents and siblings. They are learning about girlfriends, boyfriends, best friends, and fair-weather friends. They learn when friendships are on, when they are on hold, and when they are off. They learn what kind of person is good to have as a friend.

The same three elements exist in our professional friendships. We have arrived at what we know about friendships based on how we developed these concepts as children. Our friendships need time to develop and can take many forms. Learning to be there for our friends, to listen, to love, to be empathetic, and to forgive on occasion is not easy. We need to problem solve, strategize, and work on conflict resolution. We sometimes need to forgive. Expand your thinking about child and adult friendships by considering these questions:

1 Do children have different types of friends?
2 How would you describe a culture of friendship?
3 What are ways to sustain a culture of friendship?
4 What could you do to support children in developing their language of friendship?
5 Do you have a *best* professional friend?
6 How would you define a fair-weather friend?
7 What are the benefits of cultivating a culture of friendship in early childhood education?

Professional friendships are essential to our development. *New York Times* author Emma Goldberg (2022) suggests that there is an electricity to forming that first close friendship at work. Recall the times you shared laughter, giggles, and—yes—even gossip at work. Think about the tenderness you felt when you showed up to work on a rough morning and realized your friend instantly knew that something was wrong. Remember how they stepped up on that day because they recognized that you needed support. We are all worthy of this type of work friend.

You Deserve a Professional Friend!

Every educator deserves a friend, a trusted person who will support them through all the seasons of life. Bonded by trust, professional friends strive and thrive side by side while sharing both joys and struggles. As professional friends, you work on striking a balance between challenge and support. It is a reciprocal relationship as you both engage in collaborative co-development.

This book reflects a collaboration with friends who have been critical to my development. I am grateful for each and every one, as they have helped me to learn and grow. I am especially grateful to Cindy Green, one of my first and oldest professional friends, who read and edited every word on every page of this book more than once and who has offered incredible feedback. We were early-career friends and shared similar contexts. I am grateful to Dr. Hopi Martin. Through his auntie and traditional teacher, Gokoomis ("grandmother") Jacque(line) Lavallee, he belongs to the Ojibwe Marten clan. Hopi's teachings and support have deepened my awareness of the need to emphasize the term *professional friendship* over *critical friendship* for early childhood educators. In Hopi's words to me, "*critical friend* has a negative connotation because it is so linked to critique and judgment, which goes against my understanding of Anishinaabe traditional teachings." While theories of critical friendship have influenced this book, Indigenous worldviews have inspired a focus on professional friendship as a gift for all early childhood educators.

My professional friendships are different from other friendships I have. I still have friends from childhood, and I will always be grateful to them for staying with me through life. Although I cherish all my friendships, it is my professional friends who understand my professional context. They identify with my passion for early childhood education. Professional friends represent a relationship that is deliberate and complex as other friendships, and sometimes more so.

My professional friends and I share an interest in the topic of professional friendship, but it is far from the only interest we share. The term *interest* figures prominently in my pedagogical experiences in early childhood education. I used to follow themes, but now I see a curriculum as emerging from children's interests. I have an interest in exploring the concept of professional friendships. When I engage in learning and reflecting on the topic, I can make connections to children's friendships and the

Friendship in Early Childhood Education

Photo Credit: Justin Kwitco

pedagogical role of early childhood educators. These connections to practice will be featured throughout the book as provoking proposals.

The intention of this book is to demonstrate the value of professional friendships for reflection, growth, and change. It is an invitation for you to:

- Reflect on the big ideas of professional friendships.
- Consider how to apply the theories of professional friendship to practice.
- Articulate what you value in a professional friend.
- Focus on yourself to describe your own identity.
- Communicate the expectations that you have for your professional friends in your current and potential relationships.

This book offers a multilayered approach to examining friendships in early childhood education. This approach helps us recognize how important friendships are in deepening the experiences we offer to children and heightening our awareness of pedagogy and curriculum. I am using the topic of friendship to connect the layers of the early learning ecosystem. As parts of the ecosystem interact, connections among layers strengthen. Making connections is taking reflection to a higher level. To demonstrate a layered approach, I will be telling stories of friendships in early childhood education while embedding stories of my own professional friendships and layering in stories of children's friendships. Ultimately these are tales of love.

Love and Layers

Love is very much a part of my professional life and friendships. This kind of love is not familial or romantic love but professional love. I first heard this term from someone I love, who happens to be the featured friend in chapter 4, author and early childhood education expert Suzanne Axelsson. Suzanne introduced me to the research of Dr. Jools Page (2018) from the University of Sheffield on the topic of professional love, which supports the importance of close, intimate, and trusting relationships in the context of education and care. Page's research focuses on the adult-child relationship, but we can also think about professional friends as sources of love. There are many possible avenues in the quest for professional love. You can find it with children, with their families, and with professional friends. You can love materials like loose parts, and this love enhances the invitations that you provide to children. Your love can also stem from the land, from Mother Earth, who can be a great source of love. Your love can have many layers.

Layers of love in early childhood education cover you, the children, and their families with protection. Consider the metaphor of nesting dolls. My granddaughter Reese is fascinated with these dolls. Separated at the middle, each doll reveals a smaller figure inside, which has, in turn, another doll inside of it. They have endless possibilities for play and learning. For me, the dolls are an opportunity to think deeply about love, family, identity, and my chosen profession. My family comes from Romania and Ukraine, where these dolls have been popular for over a hundred years. I can imagine that my grandmother, an early childhood educator whom I never met, played with these when she was young. Nesting dolls are about carrying on a legacy from one generation to the next. A layered approach asks us to consider the stories within the stories, the nests within the nests. It is about taking care of the next generation and surrounding them with love.

What do I want to pass on to the next generation of early childhood educators and the next one after that? In turn, what will they pass on to children? In the winter season of my life, I am thinking of giving back. What will be my legacy? How will I be remembered? I have gained so much from being an early childhood educator. I want to give back to a profession that I love.

Russian American psychologist Urie Bronfenbrenner (1917–2005), who advanced the ecological theory of early childhood, is another giant on whose shoulders I stand. He described his theory as resembling nesting dolls. In

Nesting Doll Love

Photo Credit: Justin Kwitco

the center is you, layered within multiple contexts, each represented by one of the nested dolls. Your ecological system is built from interactive systems representing your direct community, then the larger community, which in turn is surrounded by the even larger sociocultural context. Imagine if you, your colleagues, the children, and their families were layered by love and support within all these systems.

Children's books about friendships are another gift to pass on to the next generation. Like nesting dolls, books support reflection. Children learn from these books. I learn from children's books too. The stories can be applied to our professional friendships. Like my grandchildren, I love Knuffle Bunny, a floppy stuffed rabbit featured in a series of books by Mo Willems. Taken together, these are the stories of main character Trixie's coming of age. From not having the language to express big feelings, to developing her first human friendship, to learning the value of giving, we watch Trixie grow through the years to become a parent herself.

Knuffle Bunny Too (2007), the second book in the series, tells the story of a friendship born from a common interest. Trixie's first friend, Sonja, has a Knuffle Bunny too! This happy happenstance leads to the friendship. The relationship between Trixie and Sonja will capture children's interest and provide inspiration to consider their own developing friendships. When children feel that they are like the characters in their stories, it supports a developing sense of self and a sense of belonging.

Trixie and Sonja's friendship helps us think about what children's and adults' peer-to-peer relationships can tell us.

1 What can we learn from observing children while they form friendships?
2 What can we learn by examining, reflecting on, and cultivating professional friendships?
3 What brings together two children or two adults to form a friendship?

The Seasons of Friendship

Spring, summer, fall, and winter. The seasons offer a perspective from which to view our lives, our friendships, and even children's play. My seasonal perspective was inspired by the teachings of the four seasons known as a Seasonal Pedagogy. It is with appreciation to Dr. Hopi Martin that I have been able to apply this Indigenous perspective to professional friendships. Hopi learned the teachings of the seasons from his auntie Jacque. The Seasonal Pedagogy (Martin 2021) relates to how children naturally learn through play, but I have come to realize that it can apply to friendships and much more.

When we consider professional friendships from a seasonal perspective, springtime represents the birth and beginnings of peer-to-peer relationships. In the summer and fall, relationships are strengthened as we move and play with friends. The fall shows us that all life and learning must come into connection to grow past the self. This is how friendships become solid and enduring relationships. The winter season represents a time to consider what happens when friendships come to an end, for whatever reason. In winter, we have time to pass on our learning, giving back to the whole community so life continues. It is also the time to tell the stories of our friendships so we can inspire other generations of early childhood educators.

The Seasonal Pedagogy is circular, cyclical, and recurrent. It is nature's inspiration for a curriculum—the content of what we teach—and pedagogy—our approach to learning. Reflecting from a seasonal perspective helped me make sense of the Ontario Ministry of Education's pedagogy for the early years, *How Does Learning Happen?*, which "is organized around four foundational conditions that are important for children to grow and flourish: Belonging, Well-Being, Engagement, and Expression. These foundations, or ways of

Reese and *Knuffle Bunny Too*!

Photo Credit: Dory Kashin Kwitco

being, are a vision for all children's future potential" (2014, 7). Before I met Hopi, I had been struggling with the four conditions, not because I didn't agree with them but because, from a teaching perspective, I couldn't figure out where to begin. When Hopi invited me to apply these conditions to the Seasonal Pedagogy, the conditions made sense as they moved cyclically with Mother Earth.

- Well-Being connects to *Birth* (spring).
- Engagement connects to *Movement* (summer).
- Belonging connects to *Relationships* (fall).
- Expression connects to *Passing* (winter).

The structure of this book has been strongly influenced by the Seasonal Pedagogy. Chapter 1 reflects the birth of professional friendships, which relates to spring and sprouting. It is about the identities that we bring to our friendships. Without embracing the self, we cannot be well. Chapters 2, 3, and 4 are about the vibrant season of summer when we engage with our friends, sharing interests and experiences. Chapter 5 represents the fall, which focuses on making connections. Finally, chapter 6 is the winter season when the seeds underground are protected, and it is time to tell the stories of our friendships. These will be stories of gratitude. From Hopi, I have learned that giving comes before taking and gratitude comes first.

Beginning with Gratitude

> *Imagine raising children in a culture in which gratitude is the first priority.* ~ Robin Wall Kimmerer

Professional friendships exist within a culture of gratitude. In a culture of gratitude, there is reciprocity as well as reciprocal relationships. Gratitude is about cultivating an ethic of fullness, that we have enough and we are enough. Gratitude reminds us that we have everything we need (Kimmerer 2013). In my life, I have the resources to support my learning and teaching in the relationships I have with my professional friends like Hopi, who is a giant in body, mind, heart, soul, and spirit. From Hopi, I learned about Indigenous, land-based, holistic pedagogies, which became a prompt for my critical reflections about friendships. The teachings of the First Peoples, who continue to care for the land I call home, remind us that it is Mother Earth who sustains us all—a perspective often missing in the white worldview. She is the ultimate early childhood educator. Mother Earth is my friend. She takes care of me, and I have a great affection for what she teaches me. Mother Earth teaches and sustains. She doesn't judge or criticize. The sun shines on everyone, and everyone can breathe her air. My heart is brimming over with gratitude for Mother Earth and for my professional friends.

Gratitude, as the state of being grateful, is an emotional response to a tangible or intangible gift. With gratitude, you acknowledge the goodness in your life in a way that helps you make connections. Gratitude is a virtue that can begin by an expression of thanks. I am grateful for and acknowledge that everywhere I step, others were here before me. My ancestors came to this land as settlers who were escaping persecution in eastern Europe. They first arrived on lands of the Kanien'kehá:ka Nation known as Montreal, in the province of Quebec, where I was born, historically a gathering place. I am thankful for the foresight and bravery of my ancestors and for my parents, Reeva and Gerald, who moved to the Toronto area when I was seven. This is where I lived until my own children were very young. Then we moved north to Richmond Hill, in York Region, the land we came to know and that knows us. This was over thirty years ago, and the surrounding forests, lakes, and rivers sustain my life. It is the land of two treaties, the Mississauga's of the Credit First Nation and the First Nations of the Williams Treaties. I respect the relationship of these nations to the land and recognize that my continued connection is through relationships. I share the responsibility to these lands and waters for my grandchildren and all other future generations. This perspective grounds my life and my work. Indigenous early childhood education perspectives are fundamental to Mother Earth and her children. It is a perspective that embraces gratitude.

The Science of Gratitude, a white paper by the Greater Good Science Center at UC Berkeley, suggests that when we practice gratitude, we become happier and more positive. We feel better. We are more satisfied and resilient (Allen 2018). I have gratitude for the words gifted to me by my professional friends that have empowered my thinking and elevated my thoughts. Gratitude can be a powerful way to grow professional friendships. There is ample research to show that gratitude helps us to initiate, maintain, and strengthen relationships. Robert Emmons, an expert on the science of gratitude, recommends that we can cultivate gratitude by keeping a gratitude journal (Emmons, Froh, and Rose 2019). Recording things for which you are grateful can also include reflections on the ways you are grateful for your professional friends. Taking your words on a page and translating them into action can be powerful. How might you express gratitude directly to your professional friends? Here are some suggestions:

- Write a note of thanks to your friend.
- Offer a small gift or token of friendship.
- Send a text or message and share your gratitude.
- Acknowledge your friend's support of your practice.

Gratitude is different from optimism, which is about *expecting* positive outcomes in life. Gratitude is about *noticing* positive outcomes in life. The benefits of gratitude apply to all, regardless of age.

Rebecca Parlakian and Sarah Barclay Hoffman (2020) of Zero to Three, an organization committed to children's healthy relationships, know about the importance of gratitude. They offer ideas for ways to model gratitude with children. I have added the last three bullet points to the list:

- By slowing down and observing children closely, you are showing your appreciation. Sharing with children what you appreciate about them provides a powerful motivator that connects and strengthens relationships.

- When you show appreciation for others, children hear words and see your actions. This demonstrates gratitude to them. You can model kindness, generosity, and gratefulness in everyday interactions with all the people you encounter.
- When you use the word *grateful*, children hear that gratitude expresses a feeling of abundance. It shows them that they are enough and that spending time together is worthy of appreciation.
- Many books written for children relate stories of thankfulness, gratitude, and generosity. Share these and encourage children to reflect on the words and meanings.
- When you model kindness, generosity, and gratefulness to Mother Earth, children learn about the importance of the land. Say thank you to the blue sky and the warm sun or whatever the day has to offer whenever you are outside with children.
- Create a gratitude documentation book with children. Record conversations and stories of gratitude. Have the children add their thoughts, pictures, or marks. Add photos and dates to journal your gratitude experiences.
- Engage in a collaborative inquiry about gratitude that sustains the interests of children over time. In this way, gratitude can become a tradition that endures beyond the inquiry.

This book is dedicated to all my professional friends, past, present, and future. Some of these relationships have stood the test of time, spanning decades! With others, all that is left are memories. Once established, professional friendships can be difficult to maintain. Still, it is with a grateful heart that I consider all the professional friendships I have had in my lifetime.

I am also grateful to you for joining me on this friendship journey. I believe that if we cultivate professional friendships, we take charge of our own professional development and personal growth. If we encourage a culture of friendship, we can support children to navigate these complex relationships. If we engage with each other, recognizing shared experiences, interests, and passions, we can become and stay friends over all four seasons, our entire lifespans!

Chapter One

Forming Friendships

THE BIRTH OF PEER-TO-PEER RELATIONSHIPS

Hello, Friend!

I am delighted to meet you! My name is Diane Kashin. I am a registered early childhood educator in Ontario, Canada. I am also a retired early childhood education professor, writing and presenting on the topic of professional friendships. I hope you don't mind my calling you "friend" in the heading of this section. You may have heard and questioned educators who refer to children as their friends. I recognize that I am risking a negative or critical reaction by saying "Hello, friend," but I want to begin this chapter in a friendly way.

As I have reflected on the practice of greeting children as friends, it has provoked deep thinking about being a friend and having a friend. In this chapter, we'll focus on the foundations of friendship. What does it mean to be a friend, to be in a friendship, and to befriend? When you are in a state of friendship, you are in a relationship with another. This requires trust, shared interests, and being self-aware. When we befriend, we can act as friends. I know that you and I are probably not friends, but I would like to challenge simplistic definitions of the term *friend*. I would like to invite you to think of the complex ways we define *friend* by reflecting on these questions:

1. Are children really friends with their teachers?
2. Should they refer to each other as friends?
3. Should I be referring to the readers of this book as my friends?
4. If we could be friends, how would our friendship start?
5. When you observe children engaging in peer-to-peer relationships, do you see parallels with your own friendships?

6. How significant are friendships to children's healthy development?
7. At approximately what age does a child begin to form their first friendships?
8. What are children doing when they form friendships?

Thinking about these questions is an example of a reflective practice, which can lead to improved outcomes for children and their families.

The Act of Reflection

Engaging in reflection supports unity within diverse groups of professionals. Professional networks and learning communities facilitate and encourage practices grounded in reflection. As your potential professional friend, I hope that you accept this invitation to reflect on the many layers of friendship within the early childhood education ecosystem.

In a parallel process, we can reflect on the development of friendships in children to spark an interest in professional friendships. We can also engage in the process in reverse. Consider these questions to support the reflection process:

1. How do children establish friendships?
2. Even toddlers can form friendships; how do they do it?
3. What social norms are used by children to make friends?

Different friendships have different norms of behavior. These norms are the implicit understandings of how we engage and behave with each other. We conform to these norms of behavior because we want to preserve the friendship. For example, with some friends, the norm is to text every day, while with others, we take weekly walks. Children's friendships are influenced by an equity norm, wherein children engage in equal sharing with each other (Paulus, Christner, and Wörle 2020). The equity norm is equally important in professional friendships, as friendship is a relationship of choice and typically egalitarian in nature.

Usually, we see children become skillful in the norms of turn-taking and sharing. We also see other friendship skills develop, such as the abilities to communicate clearly, to support, to encourage, and to protect one another. Children learn how to forgive, solve problems, resolve conflicts, listen, trust, and keep secrets. They learn to be kind, accepting, empathetic, and tolerant.

They figure out how to be loyal and how to set and respect boundaries with their friends. These skills can be cultivated so friendships can blossom. We can help children build these skills if we stop, observe, and reflect on children's proto-relationships.

A Friendship Is Born!

Photo Credit: Diane Kashin

Let's reflect more on children's friendships by considering these questions:

1 How do children maintain friendships?

2 How do children resolve conflicts in friendships?

3 How can you support children's developing friendships?

Think about a time when you, as an educator, intervened during a conflict between two friends. As conflicts among friends are inevitable, you probably have experience supporting a reconciliation among children in their peer-to-peer relationships. In your interaction with the children, you likely responded from a base of professional knowledge to help them resolve their conflict and remain friends. Did you help children recognize that friendships are equal in nature, emphasizing the equity norm? Did you help them build their friendships skills?

1. What words did you use to support conflict resolution among peers?
2. How did you respond to each child impacted by the conflict?
3. Would you change anything about the experience?

By reflecting on the actions you took in the past, you have an opportunity to consider the impact of friendships in the lives of children. Perhaps you also have begun to extrapolate the impact of professional friendships in the lives of adults via these reflections.

Imagine if we possessed all the previously mentioned skills of friendship and applied them in our professional lives. When I reflect on my professional friendships, I can see that these skills are useful and that boundary setting is particularly important. When we critically reflect on our professional friendships, we learn that we need boundaries. For example, where is the line marking the limit of time you have for your friends? A friend needs to respect your time, and you need to respect theirs. When you articulate boundaries, you learn how to assert and advocate for your needs in a way that will support your friendship. By reflecting on your boundaries, you learn more about your professional friendships.

Philosopher Donald Schön (1930–1997) explored the concept of reflective practice. He articulated the need to think about practice as a kind of artistry that continually evolves from the reflective process. Schön defined *reflective practice* as the practice by which you become aware of your implicit knowledge base and learn from your experience. To become aware of what is implicit (something implied but not plainly expressed), reflection is necessary. Schön (1987) refers to reflective practice as *reflection in action* and *reflection on action*. To reflect *in* action is to reflect while in practice, whereas to reflect *on* action involves reflecting afterward.

Examining your professional friendships and the impact they've had on your practice is reflection on action. Schön built upon the work of philosopher and educational reformer John Dewey (1859–1952), who was the first to solidly link reflection to professional learning and practice. Dewey contended that reflection in a learning context is not just a passive recall of an event. Reflection is a deliberate and active process. It is about thinking to learn.

When reflective thinking and practice are taken to a higher level, they become critical reflection. Reflecting involves observing and questioning. To be critically reflective, we seek multiple perspectives and are open to change. Taking reflection and friendship to a degree where you think and engage critically together will improve your practice. Children, families, and your professional friends will benefit, as will you.

There are many aspects of practice in early childhood education that can inspire critical reflection. One such practice is pedagogical documentation, which is intended as a tool for reflection. Defined as "making learning visible," pedagogical documentation requires deep analysis to yield an interpretation that reflects multiple perspectives and voices. Pedagogical documentation tells a story about children, including their interests, strengths, development, and ways of knowing (Dietze and Kashin 2021). An analysis of the professional friendships in your life will also tell a story. It is your story, and there are still many pages to be written. Critically reflecting on professional friendships will help you establish and maintain these relationships. This is your invitation to take your friendships to the next level. Let's start by activating our thinking.

Spheres of Friendships

Throughout the seasons of life, various factors influence our friendships. Figure 1.1 depicts the spheres or types of friendship formed by these influencing circumstances. Think about the spheres of friendship you've had in your lifetime. How significant have these relationships been to you?

Professional friends engage in shared activities. They usually have a shared interest and many aligning values. They often share a workplace.

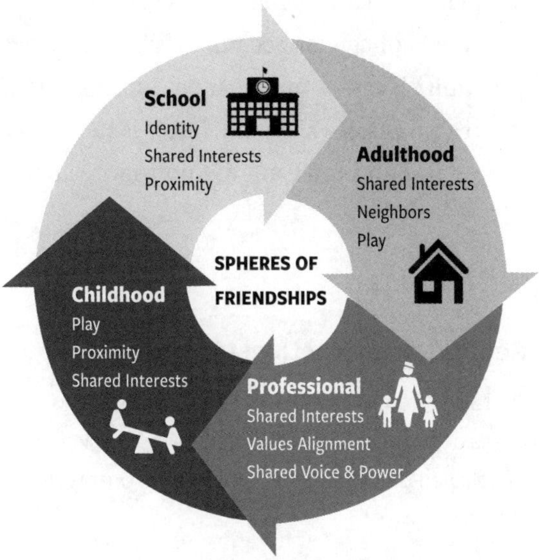

Figure 1.1
Spheres of Friendships

Professional friends are different from other friends you have in your life. Think about your friends from childhood and your later school years. You had proximity and a shared interest. You were play partners who shared! Adults usually choose friends who share interests, be it participating in a team sport, playing cards, or competing in online word games, as proximity seems less significant. Is play a common characteristic across all spheres of friendship? It should be for early childhood educators!

When you play and share materials or ideas with friends, you can reflect even as you are messing about. Play creates opportunities for respectful challenges that propel learning, especially when offered in a kind and loving way. When you observe your friends in practice, you have additional opportunities to support and challenge them on their pedagogical pathways forward.

Professional Interests

Think about your professional friends: Does playing matter, and is it part of your friendships? Do you agree with your friends about what adult play looks and feels like? One of the greatest joys of my professional life has been to facilitate play-based learning for adult students and teachers. I invite you to think about the types of play that might occur during professional learning and development and to consider their impact. Perhaps we share this interest in play-based learning for adults.

An *interest* is the state of wanting to know or learn about something. What are you interested in professionally? I think if you are reading this book, we have a common interest, or many. This is the way friendships begin! Professional friendships often occur between colleagues because of physical proximity to each other. However, proximity is not as important as interests. It is not necessary to have proximity to a professional friend, but it is necessary to share an interest. An interest is something you want to know more about. Interests are so interesting!

Making Connections to Pedagogical Practice: Interests

Almost twenty years ago, I successfully defended my doctoral dissertation about emergent curriculum. I wanted to see a change in our profession from focusing on themes to building on interests. I believed that emergent curriculum constituted an opportunity for early childhood teachers to ascend from a position of poor self-image and dubious practices to a peak of positive transformation. Delving deeply into the concept of interests has helped me learn more about what I am interested in. Lately I have been reflecting on the role that interests play in professional learning, in how children learn, and in how we learn together as professional friends. Professional friends challenge and provoke each other because they love and want what's best for each other. In this capacity, I offer you this challenge as a provoking proposal.

Provoking Proposal: Think about how you identify children's interests in practice. How do you ensure that the voices of children are represented in the interests being pursued?

When we slow down to observe and listen to children, we see interests emerge that are meaningful to their lives and friendships. If we are too quick to identify interests in children, we will not have had the time to find what interests are most meaningful to them.

In the theory of *I, Thou, It,* David Hawkins (1974) identifies shared interest as the *third* thing, or the *It* that supports the understanding of content and the development of relationships. This is the thing that is of interest to the child and to the adult. The framework of the theory is a triangle with *I, Thou,* and *It* each representing a side. On one side of the triangle, a shared interest leads to a deeper exploration of content as each learner helps the other uncover new understandings. It is the shared interest that drives the learning. Play and interests are important qualities of my professional friendships. How about yours? Do you have a friend like my friend Cindy?

Featured Friend: Cindy

Cindy is a "you've got spinach stuck in your teeth" kind of friend! I have so much gratitude for my long-lasting friendship with her. There have been times in my professional life that I've needed a friend who has the courage to tell me something that is hard to hear. I am thankful to Cindy for being able to say what needed to be said from a position of care, kindness, love, and compassion. Cindy taught me how to be a professional friend. It is through her that I have developed my own capacity to be a professional friend. She has been crucial to my professional learning. What a gift!

Diane and Cindy
Swinging in a Tree
Photo Credit: Ann MacDonald

The Power of Professional Friends

Friendships have significantly influenced my professional learning and growth. When I reflect on what I have learned about being an early childhood educator, I remember more from my experiences with friends than from any book I have read or workshop I have attended. I have learned from the stories my friends have shared too. When we tell stories as we pursue shared interests, the learning sticks. The knowledge remains with me forever.

I have grown because of the shared memories I have with my friends. Throughout my career, I have sought out friends whenever I have entered a new work context, whether a child care center, a school board, or a community college. I worked the longest at a college, teaching early childhood education, and the friendships I formed during this time have been my most intense ones. They have been a source of learning, joy, and laughter but also a source of conflict and hurt feelings. Thinking about my professional friends means reliving the heaviness of those times. At the same time, I recall the lightness of love. I have had professional friends who came into my life for only a short time. The relationships were not ongoing, and I have lost touch with them over the years. I still remember these friends fondly for all that I learned from them.

Thankfully, I am still friends with Cindy, and the bond that we share continues. It has been strong, endearing, and enduring. Our relationship is lovingly reciprocal and equal in nature because we empower each other with the gift of feedback. Receiving feedback from a friend is different from receiving it from a supervisor, where there is a power differential. When offered from a foundation of professional friendship, challenges and alternative perspectives are easier to accept. For over three decades, Cindy has challenged me to reflect, while wrapping her words in kindness and affection. A professional friend can ask provocative questions and provide different lenses to view and examine practices. A professional friend recognizes that the way they use words will impact a relationship. How you offer feedback is an important consideration on your professional friendship journey.

Borrowing from critical friendship research, we consider how feedback can be either warm or cool (Miller 2014). Warm feedback is encouraging and supportive, while cool feedback is challenging and provoking. Professional friends purposefully and knowingly provide both types of feedback to each other. When professional friends find themselves aligned in their philosophy, the pedagogical pathway forward becomes a duet. Offering feedback to our friends while on the path together can be a gift or a hinderance. Consider the following scenario.

In Your Mind's Eye

Imagine that you are returning to work in a preschool after being on leave for over a month. Your teaching partner is a friend you care deeply about. Your teaching partner is younger than you and has less experience. While you have been working at the preschool for five years, your teaching partner was hired two years ago. At that time, you were a mentor to your teaching partner, but now you believe there is more value in cultivating a professional friendship. Usually you have planned for your classes together, based on observations and analyzing the documentation. You have been away and have missed this collaboration. You learn that the children have been engaged in an inquiry about construction, evident by the display on the bulletin board. At first glance, you are not sure what to make of what is posted. You soon realize it is a good opportunity to offer warm and cool feedback to your professional friend. What would you say?

Documentation about Construction

Photo Credit: Diane Kashin

Consider the following feedback examples:

- Warm feedback: "There are so many rich opportunities for reflection here. Thank you for providing it—clearly you are programming based on children's interests. It is so wonderful to see that."
- Cool feedback: "What were the differences between the three art experiences and the children's level of engagement?"

A professional friend pays attention to the effect of their chosen words and offers feedback to empower you. Empowering others is a process of guiding them to feel and believe that they are powerful. This is true for children and adults. Empowerment, according to Liz Rouse, a lecturer in early learning, focuses on the belief that we all have strengths and capabilities. In addition, we have the capacity to become more competent (Rouse 2012). As early childhood educators, we want this for children. As early childhood educators, we should want this for our professional friends too!

Think about the power of words. Unpacking the meaning of words is a powerful tool for reflection. As professional friends, we need to cultivate a balance of power and build a relationship based on reciprocity. By stopping to reflect and consider our words, we can empower others. By choosing our words carefully, we can build positive, reciprocal professional friendships.

Big Ideas of Professional Friendships: Identity

Unpacking the meaning of the words we use in our everyday interactions with friends expands the depth and breadth of our thinking, leading to big ideas. In early learning, big ideas refer to the concepts that underpin our work. The concept of big ideas was formulated by sociologist and philosopher Jürgen Habermas (1929–). Big ideas help early childhood educators expand their knowledge, leading to improved practices and ultimately a better world. I invite you to reflect on many big ideas, as reflection leads to connections, and more ideas reveal themselves during the process. Each chapter features a big idea that is related to its focus. This chapter discusses the idea of identity.

To grow a friendship with a colleague requires that you reflect on your identity. Friendships are part of our self-identity, which is who we believe ourselves to be. Children are developing self-identity as they begin to form relationships. Making friends is a vital part of a child's emotional and social development, helping them learn about themselves. When infants begin to become aware of their own bodies, this is the earliest facet of identity. They play with their hands and feet and begin to move and notice how their bodies feel. Babies as young as one react to videos of themselves. By two years old, children can identify themselves in photographs. All the while, they are gathering information about other people as separate from themselves. Their developing senses of self also include abstract labels and descriptions applied to them by other people. Part of a child's self-identity is that they believe they are what and who others say they are. One of the first abstract labels a child attaches to their identity is their name. Heard over and over again, names as well as the labels adults give children's traits become an ingrained part of their self-images.

Think back to your own childhood. If you were to write the story of yourself as a child, what would it be? How did you learn about yourself when you were a child? One way children learn to think about themselves is through shared memories, or what is called "the remembered self." This internal picture that children construct over time is based on the stories and memories of events that adults recall with them. A narrative or story of who the child is within the context of their family is being created. This is part of the remembered self. These personal stories and memories help children understand themselves in the contexts of relationships and experiences, shaping their developing self-identities.

Closely aligned with the sense of self are children's connections to other people (including families and peer groups), places (such as their schools), and things (such as toys and other objects). As early childhood educators, we know children take personal ownership of "things" very seriously! This concept of personal possession stems from a healthy advancement in their understanding of self (Reschke 2019). Considering these facets of children's growing sense of who they are will help us be more effective in our role as early childhood educators.

Diane as a Child

Photo Credit: Unknown

What makes *you* you? Your answer includes your gender, age, race, roles, family, and life experiences. This act of reflection will help you maintain your self-identity as you come together with another in a professional friendship and establish a common identity.

1 What is important to you at your core?

2 What touches your heart and activates your brain?

3 What are your values and beliefs?

4 Who has influenced you, and why?

In their reflective practice journal *The Five Commitments of Optimistic Leaders for Children*, Judy Jablon, Nichole Parks, and Laura Ensler (2021) from Leading for Children speak of cultivating self-awareness as an essential element for leadership in early childhood education. Self-awareness is foundational to forming effective professional friendships. No matter how much you share with your friend, whether it be power, common interests, or a work context, you are still a separate being. You need to notice how your background, culture, knowledge, and experiences affect your thoughts and actions as you build relationships.

You already have the qualities that will make you a good friend to another early childhood educator. You are who you are meant to be—a loving and caring person who supports children, their families, and your colleagues. When we come together as friends, we bring our own senses of self. Then, with shared experiences, we develop a common identity. To have a successful professional friendship, our common identity should not overtake our own individual senses of self. We need to remain separate entities. Your friend can help you understand your own self because they have a close relationship with you. However, they will never know exactly what you feel.

When I think about my past professional friendships, I can now see that some of these relationships represented an unhealthy merging of identities. Imagine a Venn diagram with the overlapping area being greater than the areas that are separate. The diagram on the right in figure 1.2 is

Figure 1.2 Healthy and Unhealthy Common Identities

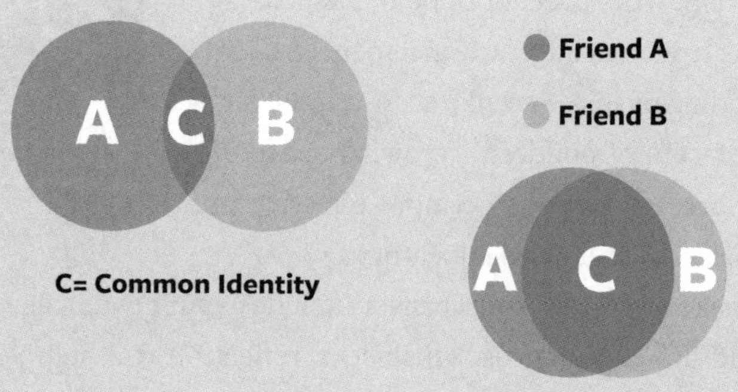

a representation of both friends losing their self-identities. Each person's individuality has diminished. Compare this relationship to a healthy relationship, shown on the left, where each person maintains their identity while cultivating a common identity related to their friendship.

Thinking Back

I had a professional friendship that lasted fifteen years. I loved my friend. She was the first person I turned to when I needed support at work, and I needed plenty of support. Our shared work context was anything but collegial. I had a difficult time navigating the toxic work environment. My friend helped me understand power dynamics and see other perspectives. We worked together, traveled together, dreamed together, and often stayed up all night talking together. When our relationship ended, I was grief-stricken. What led to the demise of our friendship? There is not an easy or concise answer to the question, as friendships are complex in nature. In the end, I felt that my identity was too strongly tied to her identity. I became more of a duo, with a common identity, and less of an individual. I felt lost and unheard. I no longer felt recognized or supported. I didn't feel that she was aware of or wanted to acknowledge my feelings. I wonder if she felt the same way about me, but I will probably never know. When I did voice concerns, she didn't want a confrontation, and our friendship ended.

Our friendship was so much a part of my identity. It was as if we were a package deal. For a long time, I had felt safe being part of this duo. We shared many memories, milestones, and interests, which aligned until they didn't. What I have learned is that it is important to be self-aware and to maintain your own identity with your professional friends. You need to trust that your professional friends will support your self-identity.

From a Basis of Trust

When you build upon a professional friendship, you do it from a position of mutual trust. Trust is critical to professional friends. Researchers Courtney Brewer, Taunya Wideman-Johnston, and Mike McCabe (2021) found that while critical friendship blurred the lines between professional and personal contexts, power imbalances hindered trust building. The model offered by the authors for developing and maintaining professional friendships positions trust at the beginning of the process. The initial step from professional indifference to tentative trust is necessary before entering into friendship.

Without trust, meaningful connection between people is impossible. *Trust* is one of the most common words in the English language but also one of the most commonly misunderstood. Let's take some time to understand the importance of trust in our professional friendships.

Researcher and educator Brené Brown (2021) offers BRAVING as an acronym to describe the elements that contribute to building and sustaining trust in relationships with friends.

Boundaries
Reliability
Accountability
Vault
Integrity
Nonjudgment
Generosity

Trust requires vulnerability and courageousness. When we distrust, we come to believe that something that's important to us is not safe with that person. Trust requires establishing *boundaries* of what is okay and what is not okay in the relationship. Trust requires that you and your friend are *reliable*. Ask yourself these three questions:

1. Can I trust that my friend will follow through on what they say they are going to do?
2. Are my friend and I able to balance competing priorities in our friendship?
3. Can I count on my friend to be consistent throughout the lifespan of our friendship?

Accountability is a necessary component of trust among friends. This one is sensitive and tender. Can you trust your friend to admit to mistakes, apologize, and make amends? Are you willing to be accountable for the mistakes you make? The *vault* refers to confidentiality. Do you hold in confidence what your friend shares with you? *Integrity* involves being courageous even when it is uncomfortable, doing what is right and not just paying lip service but embodying values.

Being *nonjudgmental* is fundamental to trust. If we feel we are not being judged, we will be more comfortable offering and asking for help from each other. Trust requires that we believe each other's intentions are good, and if we are not sure, we ask. We make assumptions and interpretations of ourselves and others in terms of words, behaviors, and actions. Extending *generosity* to our friends means that we interpret their intentions, words, and actions in the most generous way we can.

Your friend needs to know that you are committed to confidentiality in your relationship—and you should feel the same about them. You want your friend to feel safe and comfortable enough to share doubts and concerns. You can listen and reflect on how you can help your friend on their journey. You are not required to be a therapist. If you feel that your friend needs support that is beyond your comfort level, make some helpful and supportive recommendations about where your friend might get what they need. Truly listen to your friend. If a friend shares with you that a training requirement on children and trauma has triggered a memory that is stressful, you can help them find therapeutic support. A close connection to your professional friend plugs you into many opportunities to listen. Listening to our friends can change their lives.

You are not listening to respond but listening to genuinely hear the voice of your friend. Be aware of times when you deflect conversations to yourself. You may do this as a way to demonstrate that you have something in common, but often your friend needs you to focus on them instead. You can journal about it later to reflect on conversations and consider ways that you could improve your listening. Journaling helps you to get to know yourself and your relationships. A reflective journal will help you on your professional friendship journey. Start a new journal to chronicle your professional friendships. When you write your answers to the following questions in your journal, reflect on why they appear in the order that they do.

1. Who are you?
2. Are you willing to give the gift of professional friendship to another?
3. Who might you approach to be a professional friend?
4. What makes them approachable?
5. Who do you know who would benefit from your support and friendship?
6. Will you benefit by giving your time to be a professional friend?
7. What do you think your friend needs from you?
8. Will your friendship stand the test of time?

Suzanne Degges-White (2018) is a counselor and professor. She categorizes our friendship choices into two main factors: individual and environmental. Individual factors include approachability/social skills, closeness, similarity, and self-disclosure. Environmental factors include life events, activities, geography, and proximity. Both factors have come into play in my friendships. To achieve a lasting friendship, balancing individual and environmental factors is essential.

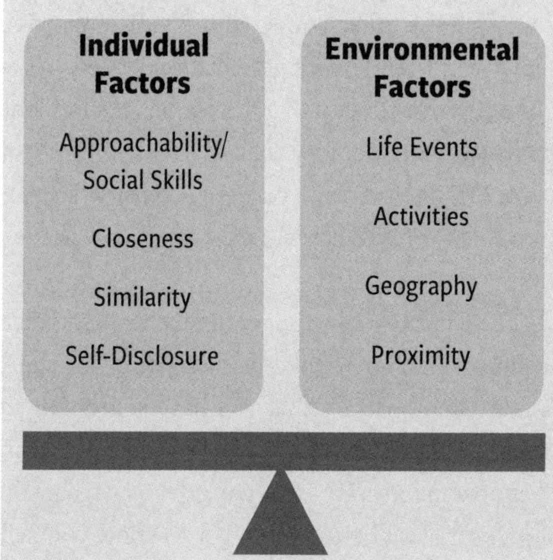

Figure 1.3 Categorizing Friendship (Degges-White 2018)

When I first met Cindy, we sat on a number of committees together. Our friendship grew because she was approachable. She had good social skills and seemed genuinely interested in growing our friendship. She shared positive and kind words, an act that generates feelings of familiarity and closeness. I wanted to be around Cindy because she made me feel good about who I was, what I believed, and what I enjoyed doing. She supported the aspects of my professional identity that mattered to me. She listened to me. With Cindy, I felt like I had a voice, and I continue to feel this way.

Do you have a friend who gives you what I have received from Cindy: mutual trust, respect, and affection? Someone who is both a sounding board and a champion? Perhaps you have a potential friend you can approach to take your relationship to another level. A potential new professional friend could be someone you just met who is open and approachable or an existing

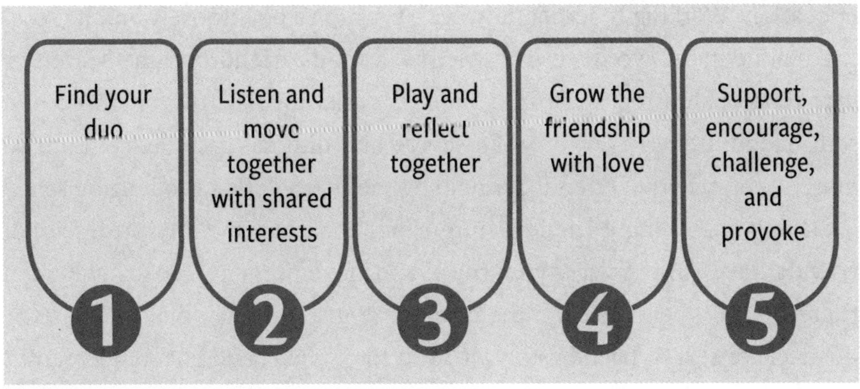

Figure 1.4 Five Steps to Professional Friendships

friend who has the potential to become a pedagogical partner. Forming a dynamic duo is the first step to a professional friendship. As reflected in figure 1.4, five steps are involved.

Along the way, consider your answers to the following questions about your dynamic duo:

1 What can you learn from your friend?
2 What can your friend learn from you?
3 What can you do together to further your shared interests?
4 Do you have time to play? What will you play with?
5 Are your warm feelings toward your friend growing as you move together?
6 How might your friendship grow?
7 What feedback can you offer your friend about an area of practice that would benefit from growth?
8 What feedback would you like your friend to offer you? Is there something you are struggling with?

Thank You for Being a Friend

The most significant professional decision I've made was to retire early from a position coveted by others. It was not easy. I was worried about leaving a former friend behind. We vowed to stay friends and find ways to collaborate. For about a year after I retired, we presented workshops, wrote, and dreamed together about empowering possibilities for early childhood education. Working together, however, proved to be intensely and increasingly difficult, as we were competitive, and my friend became secretive. The relationship fell apart in a time of social media. I was blocked and unfriended. It was over. It was a severe and difficult experience. I am so grateful for my other friends for helping me through this challenging time.

Having and being a friend is important for everyone. My professional friends have supported my learning and development. Most have been there for me when I needed them to be. When you must make significant life decisions, your friends stay with you for support and encouragement. I am grateful to each and every one of my professional friendships, those that endured and even the ones that ended. To end this chapter, I posed four questions to Cindy, whom I recognize as my first and oldest professional friend who has endured. I hope you are as inspired by her words as I am.

Four Questions for My Friend: Cindy

1. **After reading the chapter, what sparked your interest?**

   I accepted your invitation to think more intently about the values that are important to me when in a professional friendship. The terms *like-mindedness* and *respectfulness* are often used when we think about close and harmonious relationships between people. But to me these attributes present as too open-ended, since each of us has unique thoughts about how we would or expect to see evidence of these values. Diane, our shared thinking about the valuable role that early childhood educators play in the lives of young children and their families is at the core of our relationship. I too am proud to be an early childhood educator. Feeling comfortable enough to share and play with ideas is something I value. Over the years, I developed and balanced a work ethic that fueled my passion for this profession. Thinking more specifically, these are the values that enabled me to gravitate toward pursuing a professional relationship with you, Diane. We continue to share and nurture these values—they certainly have sustained the test of time!

2. **As you considered this spark/interest, how has your thinking moved with it?**

   Thinking about shared values led me to realize that I have expectations when it comes to my professional relationships. Having a mutual understanding about our relationship's code of ethics is essential. Again,

Diane, our trust in each other enables us to articulate our expectations and aspirations. I am also playing with the thought that not all professional friends are critical friends.

3 **After considering questions one and two, what connections are you making to your own experiences with professional friends?**

Now that I am retired from our profession, I no longer have the same experiences with my professional friends. Over the years, and fortunately for me, many of my professional friends have grown to become personal friends too, so our relationships will continue to evolve. I will always be an early childhood educator, and my heart will continue to be open to children, their families, and other educators!

4 **What advice can you give to the readers of this book to help them on their journeys with professional friends?**

Begin with your self-image. Do you see yourself as a competent and capable early learning educator? Pursue and work at developing mutually respectful professional relationships, even if that means starting with one other person. Avoid being competitive. Seek support. Be yourself. Keep yourself informed of pedagogical issues and topics that intrigue and excite you. I extend my gratitude to Diane as I, as well as many others, continue to enrich my thinking and practice due to her endless sharing of her intellectual prowess. Enjoy the journey!

—Cindy Green

Chapter Two

Forging Friendships

ENGAGING THE HEART

Hello, Friend!

How are you doing? I am asking because I care. This chapter is about bringing your heart to your relationships with friends. It is about engaging with your friends so that the relationships become stronger and can withstand the test of time. Friends should feel like they belong together. Our friends feel like coming home and help us feel a sense of belonging. Friendships and belonging are fundamental human needs. This chapter is about friends who feel like family because the heart is so strongly involved. It is about the languages of friendships, listening to our emotions, and listening to our friends. It is about cultivating a common identity with friends by aligning our values. Know that once you have formed a friendship, you can make it stronger, forging it into something that can last a lifetime. Your friend might be the reason you get up in the morning and go to work!

Having a best friend at work is one of the main reasons people stay at their jobs. Friendships are vital for fulfillment and satisfaction at work. Work is a primary place where friendships are made, maintained, and solidified. When you are in the trenches with others at work, it's an opportunity to build deeper bonds. The early 2020s were not easy on friendships as the pandemic affected many areas of our lives, including friendships. Friendships that were characterized by getting together after work had to shift online. Yet isolation can lead to reflection. After hours and hours of thinking about my professional relationships—those that endured and those that ended—I realized that I couldn't live without my professional friends.

The pandemic put many relationships, including friendships, under pressure and scrutiny, and the effects will linger for years. Think about your pandemic friendship experiences. How did your friendships weather the storm? If you worked in child care during the pandemic, you really felt the storm. While everyone was in the same storm, we were not all in the same boat. What I went through during the pandemic pales in comparison to the experiences of early childhood educators working directly with children. The world cannot operate without child care: it is an essential service that keeps the economy functioning. Those who rock the cradle were there for all of us, loving and nurturing children during a pandemic that rocked the world. Working from home was not an option. Working during an isolating, precarious time while feeling fraught with worry about their own and everyone else's health and well-being was a feat of strength and fortitude.

Many professional friendships grew during the COVID crisis. Early childhood educators were on the frontlines of the pandemic, and being together in the trenches strengthened many bonds. I haven't always been comfortable with the term *frontline* to describe early childhood educators, but it now seems apt. The dictionary defines *trenches* as a place or situation in which people do very difficult work together. While some friendships during COVID nurtured a sense of belonging and became stronger, others faltered.

Did COVID change your friendscape? A *friendscape* is the landscape of your friendships. If your friendscape looks different now, it is because traumatic experiences have a way of destabilizing social networks. Author Kate Murphy (2021) wrote about rearranging friendscapes in the post-pandemic world, explaining that instinctively we gravitated toward friends who offered comfort and support. Without conscious thought, we may have withdrawn from friends who dragged us down. When you decided not to return texts or join group chats, you may have slowly shrunk the breadth of your friendscape. The pandemic helped put a definitive end to certain friendships, and it allowed others to simply peter out in ghostly whimpers.

Think about how you might grow and cultivate the friendships that endured or became stronger during this difficult time.

1. Which of your professional friendships thrived during the pandemic years?
2. Why do you think these friendships became stronger?
3. How might you continue to cultivate these friendships?
4. What effect did these friends have on your professional life during the pandemic?
5. What gifts of support did your professional friends give you during this time?

6 What did you talk about with these professional friends?

7 Did any of your professional friendships fade during this time?

8 Why do you think friendships end?

In the absence of shared social spaces, including offices, coffee shops, parties, and gyms, some of your relationships may have revealed themselves to be friendships of convenience. With friendscapes adjusted during the pandemic, there was, according to Murphy, a great friendship reckoning. Did this happen to you? Reckoning involves being calculating about your friendships. Consider these questions as you analyze your professional relationships:

1 Did you become closer to a friend from work because you faced the stress of working on the frontlines together during the pandemic?

2 If these relationships became stronger, was it harder to maintain friendships with others who did not share the same work context?

During this time of social isolation, I was very fortunate that one of my cherished professional friends lives only ten minutes away. During the pandemic, it seemed odd to meet with Rosalba virtually, but we needed to stay in touch! As the world slowly opened up, it became easy once more to get together, sharing delicious meals while having deep pedagogical dialogues. Rosalba knows my history. Rosalba shares my context; we both began as early childhood educators working in child care. We share this social identity. We share interests, passions, conversations, and laughter! I trust Rosalba, and I am very grateful for our relationship.

Featured Friend: Rosalba

I love teaching and keeping in touch with students after they have graduated. When Rosalba was looking for a mentor, a mutual friend—my former student who was her professional friend—thought of me. We met for dinner, and we connected. Our relationship evolved into a professional friendship. We learn from each other, enjoy each other's company, and share a common pedagogical identity. Together we are candid and expressive. We never run out of things to say. We don't hold back, and often we talk over each other—though we are working on listening without interrupting! The difficult questions we ask each other are wrapped in trust, respect, and love.

Rosalba and Diane in the Studio

Photo Credit: John Bortolotti

Friendships Take Time and Effort

The comfort of having a friend may be taken away, but not that of having had one. ~ Seneca the Younger

During the years that I have been friends with Rosalba, she has married, had three children, and operated the Acorn School, a Reggio-inspired child care center, which was only minutes away from my home. Spending time there was joyful. When Rosalba decided to close the school, I was there for her, and I was there for her while she navigated the next stage of her working life. She has been there for me during the many transitions of my life. One of the main reasons for the endurance of this friendship with its age difference is that we became more like family. No matter what we were facing over the years, ending our friendship was never an option.

Our friends can be in different seasons of their lives. One friend may be in the retirement phase of life while the other is starting a new and demanding position. The latter is in the springtime of life and the former is in the winter season. I know why my friendship with Rosalba has endured and why other significant friendships did not. Whatever season of our lives we are experiencing, we work on our relationship. It was and continues to be a reciprocal priority.

Thinking Back

During the time that my friendship with my former friend ended, I was experiencing many life-changing challenges. I retired early because I wasn't happy, but the role had become a part of my identity. I wanted to continue working in this next phase of life, which also included moving, another significant life transition. I was very anxious and afraid of the unknown. I was questioning my own identity. While I tried to share my feelings with my friend, she seemed focused on her own challenges and stress. At the time, I had only a handful of professional friends. I didn't want our friendship to end. When it did, I was filled with remorse, regret, and profound sadness. I couldn't stop thinking about my friend. It consumed me for years. Where did I go wrong? I was dwelling on what had happened and replaying all the events and conversations that led to the demise of our relationship. I have since learned to forgive, and now I can look back with kindness, acceptance, and love. I can focus on what I learned from my friend and recognize how it helps me to be in the present, not just in the past. In the present, I am learning about my identity. I can now tell the story without regret. I can remember my friend from a place of gratitude.

In the years that I was focused on the past, I was living in regret. It was a difficult place to be, and I am grateful for my professional friends because they helped me to accept the past and move on. It is through these relationships that I keep reflecting and improving. Cindy will always be my first professional friend who lasted. I have such gratitude for Rosalba that it feels almost overwhelming! She has always been there for me, without hesitation, often with some delicious delicacy in hand. If we have differences, we talk them out by sharing where we are in our lives. With Rosalba, I feel the connection with my heart. With Hopi, the connection is with my spirit. He is featured in chapter 3. In chapter 4, where I feature my friend Suzanne, the connection is with my mind. I am very grateful to be moving with these professional friendships holistically. I am grateful that my friends listen to me, and I am working on a being a better listener for them.

Listening to Our Emotions

Listening, being open, and talking are essential to maintaining relationships. As early childhood educators, we help children express their feelings to support their emotional intelligence. We know how important the ability to perceive, control, and evaluate emotions is to children. Internationally known psychologist Daniel Goleman (1995) put the spotlight on emotional intelligence, focusing on how our two minds—the rational and the emotional—together shape our destiny. Emotional intelligence means having the skills and ability to understand, utilize, and manage one's own feelings. It includes the capacity to be aware of and respond to the feelings of others. Reflecting on your emotional intelligence is also beneficial in your exploration of friendships in early childhood education.

While emotional intelligence is shaped by our early childhood experiences, it is not fixed early in life. Children and adults can develop the emotional intelligence they need to thrive and succeed in friendships and other relationships. We can learn how to understand and manage stress, anxiety, and frustration. We can develop a tool kit to manage our big feelings. Goleman and Richard Boyatzis (2017), a professor known for his work with emotional intelligence, categorized it into four domains: self-awareness, self-management, social awareness, and relationship management. Nested within each domain are twelve *competencies* that we can learn, reflected in table 2.1.

Self-Awareness	Self-Management	Social Awareness	Relationship Management
Emotional awareness	Emotional self-control Adaptability Achievement oriented Positive outlook	Empathy Organizational awareness	Influence Coach and mentor Conflict management Teamwork Inspirational leadership

Table 2.1 Emotional Intelligence Domains and Competencies

My feelings about my past friendships run the gamut from warm and fuzzy to agitated and intense. Sometimes I can't shake the anxious feelings or big emotions attached to some friendships. My reaction to them is strong, and I am intensely sad, angry, or both. These are powerful emotions, and at times they are out of proportion to the situation that caused the feelings. These big feelings are not healthy, and they are the result of a powerful professional relationship that is not or was not working.

Early learning and care is a relationship-driven profession that requires collaboration with others. What happens when those collaborations go sour and big emotions take hold? Early childhood educators are trained to respond to the unique developmental needs and emotions of young children. This requires effort, knowledge, and skills—most critically, the skills of emotional intelligence. Once again, we can reflect on how we help children manage their emotions while learning how to deal with our own, in a parallel process. When children are in the midst of big feelings, it is difficult for them to play. It is the same for their teachers. Managing our stress and anxiety leaves us more energy for learning.

Donna Housman (2022), author of "Even Superheroes Need Support: Emotional Intelligence for Early Childhood Educators," reminds us that young children are emotional detectives. Children develop in the context of relationships, and emotion is a child's first language. With their absorbent brains, they have the capacity to recognize stress in others by observing the reactions and responses of the key adults in their world. They can only become fluent in the skills of emotional intelligence if their teachers are modeling and guiding. To do this, we must first build our own emotional toolboxes. We need the support of others so that we, in turn, can help children develop their own toolboxes to carry throughout their lifespans.

Professional friends can help fill our toolboxes with training, mentoring, and coaching. Prioritizing our emotional well-being supports building an infrastructure of mental health. Talking about feelings with our professional friends is critical. Children and adults with higher emotional intelligence can focus better, are more engaged and more empathetic, and have more positive relationships (Tominey et al. 2017). If we model emotional intelligence in our own relationships, we can be more effective in supporting its development in children.

Part of building an equitable ecosystem is nurturing our own emotional well-being and professional satisfaction. For Housman (2022), this means ensuring that every early childhood educator has the respect, professional training, and systemic support they need. In turn, they can help every child realize their potential.

1. What can you do as a friend to co-construct a parallel process for developing emotional intelligence?
2. How do you show respect to your professional friends?
3. Are there additional ways you could show respect?
4. What is the role of professional friends in professional learning, training, and growth?
5. What strategies have you used to support children's emotional intelligence?
6. In what ways could these same strategies be applied to professional relationships?
7. What do you need to do to support the well-being of professional relationships?
8. How do you know when a friend is feeling stressed?

Listening to Our Friends

Talking is a healthy way to maintain friendships, especially ones experiencing change. If you are committed to growing a professional friendship, listening to your friend is key. French philosopher Emmanuel Levinas (1905–1995) believed that at the core of our personal ethics are human interactions and that listening, and the understanding and empathy it engenders, will give our lives meaning and direction (Murphy 2020). Listening is everything in professional friendships!

A good listener makes the effort and takes the time to help a friend find their voice. They are open to receiving what their friend is saying, and they understand that life changes will inevitably shake up their relationships. What happens when your professional friend gets a promotion, retires, finds a new friend, or takes up a new interest? What can we do to keep our professional friends? If we focus on talking, being open, and listening in our professional friendships, we can overcome so much. Throughout all the changes that I have experienced in my life and all the changes my friend Rosalba has experienced, we continue to share a passion for early childhood education.

A good listener embraces silence. Silence is the absence of intentional sound. There is a science of silence that shows us why it's healthy for us to embrace it. Researcher Ron Valle (2019) lists the many health benefits of silence, including mental and emotional stability, intuitiveness, conflict resolution, healing, and spiritual awareness. Silence actually is a superpower!

Yet silence can be unsettling. Silence forces us to notice our thoughts, which can shine a light on our fears and insecurities and make us feel a need to fill in the silence. Listening is often more valuable than speaking. Listening plugs you into life and recharges your batteries. It helps you understand yourself as much as the other person. According to Murphy (2021), hearing is not the same as listening. When we listen, we hear more than what is said, as we are making meaning of the messages being expressed. Listening happens when someone takes an interest in who you are and what you are doing, being mindful not to listen only to respond. We succeed as listeners when the other person feels like we totally get what they are trying to say. They may think or tell us directly, "Yes, that is exactly what I meant." A good listener tries not to get bogged down by their own thoughts and superficial judgments. A good listener picks up on the subtext of what people are saying. As early childhood educators, we can offer the gift of listening to our professional friends.

You will never arrive at a time when you can honestly say you listen perfectly in every situation. However, every aspect of your life will be affected if you make listening a goal. Author Nancy Kline (2020) suggests that we are all guilty of interrupting. What if we told our professional friends that they were free to speak and we would not interrupt? My former friend often finished my sentences. I remember being so frustrated. I think she assumed she knew what I was going to say. She was often wrong. It is unnerving to be interrupted and have sentences completed by others who presume they know what we are going to say. Sometimes I do stumble and fumble on words, but with a little patience, I can complete my train of thought. Having your thinking interrupted is so destructive that it weakens friendships and makes decision-making difficult. Imagine having a professional relationship with a friend that is without interruption. Keeping a promise of no interruption is not easy, but it is worth trying. Rosalba and I often speak over each other because we are excited to share the thoughts that are sparked in our conversations. The conversations in which we work on listening are deeply reflective, powerful, and energizing. We are making listening a friendship goal.

I have had many adventures with Rosalba, including three study tours to Reggio Emilia, Italy. Shortly after visiting Reggio Emilia in 2006, Rosalba

Professional Friends in Reggio Emilia
Photo Credit: Unknown

and I helped bring *The Hundred Languages of Children* exhibit to Toronto. The shared experience had a profound effect on our identities. We are both influenced by this philosophy that understands teaching as relationship (Malaguzzi 1993). Being within the space that housed the exhibit meant learning together with professional friends. The learning and the relationships are intertwined, as is identity. It takes work to consider who we are as individuals and to know what we can offer others.

Inspired by my experiences with the exhibit and in Reggio Emilia, and by dialogue with friends, I can see what may be possible for all children, their families, and teachers. I am appreciative of the shoulders of giants on which I stand. However, it is time that we shape our own identities and be our own giants. We need to empower ourselves to believe that each of us has the potential to affect the pedagogical practice of the early learning community now and in the future.

The Languages of Professional Friendships

Surviving Female Friendships: The Good, the Bad, and the Ugly by Nicole Zangara (2012) relates friendships to love languages. The five love languages of affirmation, acts of service, gifts, giving quality time, and physical touch are usually connected to romantic relationships. Relating love languages to professional friendships will help strengthen your relationships. You don't have to speak the same love language as your friends; you just have to make space for differences and understanding, which requires listening (Noll 2019).

Our friends are all individuals with their own identities, and our relationships with them are unique. Which professional friend would you go to first if you were feeling sad? Whom would you seek if you wanted a deep conversation about your practice? Your choices may have to do with their love languages. Friends who offer *words of affirmation* find it easy to express their love. They offer words of affirmation when they say "I miss you" or "I am thinking of you." For some friends, actions speak louder than words, and their language is *acts of service*. If this is your friend's love language, they might not offer expressions of love but will show up for you with support and encouragement. Another language of love is the *giving and receiving of gifts*. The gift doesn't have to be material or expensive. It can be something your friend makes, sees, or finds that makes them think of you. *Quality time* is a language of love that values making time to go out to eat, grab a coffee, or go for a walk together. Finally, there is the language of *physical touch*. Do you have friends who are great huggers? Not all your friends will be comfortable with this expression of love. Not everyone likes hugs because not everyone speaks the same love language. What are the languages of your professional friendships? Can you see beyond words to their meanings, as the poet and philosopher Henry David Thoreau once expressed?

> *The language of friendship is not words*
> *but meanings.* ~ Henry David Thoreau

In Your Mind's Eye

Imagine you have arrived at work on a Monday. Your teaching partner is a professional friend. She is excited to show you a curated collection of cardboard. She is talking quickly and is animatedly describing where the materials can be placed. When you look at the cardboard collection, it makes you a little uneasy. It has not been sorted. You are not sure what the possibilities might be, and you would like to explore the cardboard first. You worry that there might be too much, which could be overwhelming for the children. What might you say to your friend?

As a professional friend, you want to respond in a way that expresses your warm and loving feelings in your particular love language. You also want to respond in a way that provokes thinking. Responding in these ways demonstrates empathy. Empathy is the ability to sense the emotions of others, coupled with the ability to imagine what someone else might be thinking or feeling. Vecchi (2010) speaks of empathy as a relationship that people have with their environment, a kind of thread that connects. Materials have languages too. The languages of materials are influenced by their affordances, or what they have to offer the user. Not all materials "speak" the same way, and they can be "heard" differently. It is the same with our professional friends.

Consider the following feedback examples:

- Warm feedback: "Your excitement is infectious, and it makes me smile with gratitude that I get to work with you."
- Cool feedback: "How might these materials be organized so that children are invited to notice, pause, and explore the languages of cardboard? How might we invite children to act on these materials to release their creative potential?"

Making Connections to Pedagogical Practice: The Languages of Learning

Materials are active participants in young children's learning (Penfold 2019). When we listen to the languages of materials as adults, we see these possibilities more fully. When we are captivated by the beauty and potential of materials, it has a spillover effect on the children.

Provoking Proposal: If you place intentionally chosen materials on an overhead projector to create a scene on the wall, what do you think children will do with this invitation?

The space is designed to engage and express. Will children be inspired to respond? Will children move the materials around? Will they experiment with color, light, and texture like artists? When children have the opportunity to respond to an invitation that empowers them with the agency to create, they feel valued.

When we take time to be with materials in responsive spaces and listen to their languages, we can see possibilities for children. Can you create a place within your context that activates exploration and inspires children and your friends to be expressive? What materials might be in that space? How might the materials be organized to invite exploration?

Professional Friendship and Self-Doubt

A friend is there for you when you have doubts or concerns about yourself. We all have these moments! Can you recall a time when you doubted yourself? I have had many of these moments, and it is emotionally difficult to conjure up these memories. I internalized my feelings of doubt and was afraid to share them. The psychological term associated with these feelings is *imposter syndrome*, a persistent internalized fear of being exposed as a fraud. Some very successful people experience feelings of not being worthy of praise or success. Imposter syndrome is often associated with overachievement and perfectionism. If you can relate to the feeling of being a fraud, you are in good company.

Have you ever felt like an imposter? Knowing this about yourself is important because it will impact your practice and your relationships. Not everyone feels like a fraud. Cindy did not experience these feelings in her working life, but I did. Other friends have shared these feelings, as we often make the topic of feeling like a fraud part of our professional exchanges. Do you trust your friends enough to have a conversation about self-doubt? Do your friends trust you? More important, do you trust yourself?

If you have difficulty trusting yourself, it may be that you are disconnected from your feelings. This may be especially true for those who grew up in families where their feelings were ignored. You may overanalyze situations, which gets in the way of your ability to listen to your body and your emotions. You may live in a state of doubt where it is easier to believe more in others than in yourself. Yet you likely doubt yourself more than others do.

When I was growing up, I felt that my father lauded my older brother but left little time for me. This childhood emotional neglect may be responsible for my experiences with imposter syndrome. It also motivates me to foster self-trust. You can do the same by tuning into your feelings. With acceptance, you can learn to trust and be in relationships with professional friends.

Discounting your feelings sets you up to doubt yourself. And doing so may leave no room for your friends to really understand you. The opportunity to work through any issues and deepen your trust and friendship will be lost. When you accept your feelings and work toward understanding them better, you will be more able to trust. Taking stock of your emotions will give you a clearer picture of your relationships, your strengths, your challenges, and your preferences. Listen to your emotions and honor the messages they are telling you. Your emotions should not be a burden but rather serve and protect you.

The persistent fear of being exposed as a fraud is often associated with higher rates of burnout, job dissatisfaction, and stagnancy. Know that the key to coping with imposter syndrome is communication. Share your feelings with your professional friends. You and your friends may be relieved to find out that you are not alone. Author Lindsay Kolowich Cox (2020) offers these nine strategies to cope with imposter syndrome, illustrated in figure 2.1:

Know the signs	Is it hard for you to accept praise? Do you apologize when you didn't do anything wrong? Do you fear failure and have very high standards?
Know you are not alone	Even those considered highly accomplished can have imposter syndrome. There are many among us.
Distinguish humility and fear	Can you find a healthy balance between feeling worthy and feeling entitled? You can be humble about your accomplishments or overcome with fear because of them.
Let go of perfectionism	The need to be perfect is unrealistic and feeds imposter syndrome. Perfectionism is counterproductive and will make you feel even more like a fraud.
Be kind to yourself	Extend kindness to yourself. Don't listen to the voice in your head saying you are not enough. Replace negative self-talk with positive self-talk.
Track your success	You have had a role in your own success. Document your accomplishments.
Talk to a mentor or friend	Sharing your thoughts and experiences with someone else will make you better equipped to deal with your imposter syndrome.
Say yes to opportunities	Do you have too much on your plate, or are you saying no because you feel you can't do it because you're not worthy? Know that this is your imposter syndrome speaking.
Embrace the feelings	It is hard to get rid of imposter syndrome completely. Recognize the feelings and stop it from hindering your success.

Figure 2.1 Ways to Cope with Imposter Syndrome

Pay attention to how you talk about your professional life to yourself and others. If you find that acknowledging your own success or receiving praise from others feels uncomfortable, do some reflective thinking, because these thoughts may be negatively affecting your professional life. If you are overcome with the feelings associated with imposter syndrome, you will not be able to be the best professional friend you can be. If you experience imposter syndrome, you may need to devote time to nurture yourself, emotionally and spiritually. You may need to prioritize time for professional friendships that empower you to be your best self as these friends will help you overcome feeling like an imposter.

Professional Friends Empower

Relationships with professional friends can be empowering as long as one friend does not always seem more powerful than the other. When it comes to making mutual decisions, if one friend is paying deference to the other, then the relationship might be something other than a professional friendship. If you feel more powerful in the relationship, perhaps you are taking on a mentor role. If you feel less powerful or powerless in the relationship, perhaps you are acting as a mentee. A mentor is more powerful than a mentee. A mentor is the one sharing and using their knowledge. A mentee is there to receive. Professional friends know that to achieve a relationship that is equal in nature, each friend works on empowering the other.

I have been a mentor to many, and I hope that I was a friendly adviser who did not contribute to negative feelings. But in these relationships, there was a power differential. The mentees deferred to my skills, expertise, and experience. When I have been mentored, I've felt empowered at times, but I have also felt the opposite. As I mentee, I have experienced feelings of having surrendered my power and voice. Reflect on these different relationships to better understand yourself and your friendships.

Professional friendships that endure will experience a natural ebb and flow spurred by the power that comes with professional knowledge and experience. At times, one friend may be leading, the other following. Professional friends empower because rather than telling each other how to do something, they walk respectfully alongside each other, holding each other's hands and offering support on their journeys. In your partnership, you share power. You pass power. At times, you accept direction and advice. At other times, you offer it, depending on your knowledge and experience. You are aware of the value of empowerment as friends and partners.

1. Are you willing to be a partner and hold another's hand on a long journey forward?
2. When you think of yourself as a professional friend, can you see yourself as both a leader and a follower?
3. Can you be a mentor and a mentee at any given time with your friend?

A professional friend volunteers to be in this relationship as an opportunity to pay forward their hard-earned professional experience and wisdom. At times, your focus will be on the goals and aspirations of another. At other times, the focus will be on you.

When you focus on another person, you recognize the potential of your words to empower. The words we use with our professional friends should be carefully chosen if we want to encourage and support growth. What words would you use to frame feedback that is both warm and cool, encouraging and challenging? Start by listening to your friend without interruption and then frame what you say as a supporting response, not a shifting response.

- A *shifting response* is self-promoting or qualifying.
- A *supporting response* is positive, thoughtful, and encouraging.

A supportive response shows that you care about your friend. Be a good listener by taking the time and effort to help your friend find their voice. Murphy (2021) suggests it will be like a dance. With a good listener, you are dancing in sync. When you are in conversation with a weak listener, it is like dancing with someone who is keeping a different rhythm or who has no rhythm.

As a professional friend, be a listener who is trying to understand another point of view. If your friend discloses that they are rethinking their practice of featuring calendar time in their morning meetings with children, your response would be shifting if you said, "I keep a calendar in the room, but we don't use it during group gatherings. That practice is so outdated." A supporting response would ask thoughtful questions such as, "What led to your new thinking?" After listening, you can offer an encouraging and positive statement such as, "Your reflections are very interesting and show that you are thinking deeply about your practice."

When we are able to think beyond our own needs and instead become completely absorbed in thinking about and acting with someone else's needs in mind, we engage in the act of decentering. *Decentering* is a process of stepping outside ourselves to move beyond the self. What would be the effect on our friends if we decenter our responses? With professional friends, the goal is to focus on another and learn about your commonalities and differences. Rosalba and I are different in many ways. I am older and my ancestry is Ashkenazi Jewish from eastern Europe. She is Catholic and her ancestors are from southern Italy. What connects us is our common identity as early childhood educators with shared passions and interests. Identity is how we view ourselves (our self-image) as well as what we are passionate about. Applying a Venn diagram to a professional friendship can help us identify our common identity. When we see where we intersect, we can grow our friendship in meaningful and mutually beneficial ways. Figure 2.2 depicts the intersection of the common identities and passions shared by Rosalba and me.

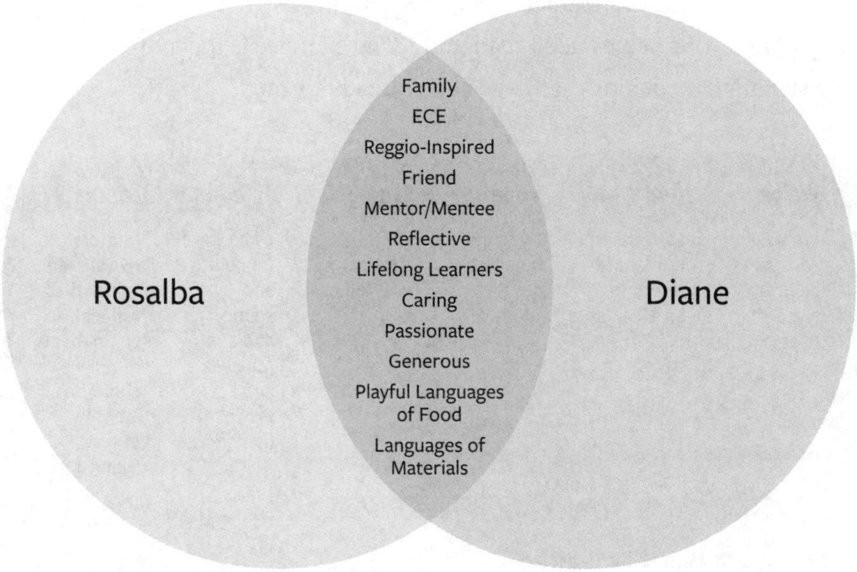

Figure 2.2 Identifying Common Identities

A Venn diagram exercise can also help you to see how you and your friend are different. Accepting differences is important to cultivating professional friendships. My former friend was an introvert. I am an extrovert. During the time we were friends, I felt that she wanted me to be more like her. I did not feel accepted for who I was. Over the course of our friendship, our values no longer seemed to be in alignment.

Big Ideas of Professional Friendships: Values

Sharing values with your professional friends is important. According to Carlina Rinaldi, president of Reggio Children and professor of pedagogy at the University of Modena and Reggio Emilia, values represent "the ideals that a person aspires to in his or her life." In Reggio Emilia, the school is described as a place "where values are transmitted, discussed, and created" (Rinaldi 2021, 101). Transmitting, discussing, creating, and strengthening values is important because we are diverse in racial and cultural backgrounds, education levels, and professional experiences.

What values are at the core of your practice? What values are at the core of your friend's practice? Do your values align? Professional friends have unique and separate identities, but they intersect with a common identity of aligned values, which represents the big idea of this chapter. In figure 2.3, the "values jar" exercise demonstrates a way to discuss values with a professional friend. Revisit values throughout the lifetime of your relationship, especially during life transitions for you or your friend, as these will be times when your values need realigning. The exercise is meant to help forge and sustain friendships that have been already formed.

Write ▶	Ask ▶	Place ▶	Shake ▶	Discuss ▶	Identify
out your core values on little strips of paper.	your friend to identify four or five core values on strips of paper.	the strips of paper into the values jar.	the jar and take out one value at a time.	using warm (encourage and support) and cool (challenge and provoke) feedback.	four or five shared values that will be components of the common identity of your friendship.

Figure 2.3 The Values Jar Exercise

When Rosalba and I tried the "values jar" exercise, we identified the common core values of our friendship. Together we value

- play
- relationships
- reflection
- inspiration
- each other

Rosalba and Diane
Align Values
Photo Credit: Diane Kashin

Your values are what are important to you. You can have different values than your friend. Just as our values guide our own actions, understanding a friend's values helps us navigate the relationship through the difficult times. Using the values jar, you have the opportunity to talk through values that do not align. This communication is essential if the friendship is going to last.

Thank You for Being a Friend

I have no doubt that my friendship with Rosalba will endure. Our relationship has transcended to the level where we feel like family. We are connected deeply through our hearts. She is like the sister I never had. As an expression of our friendship love language, I gifted *Stick and Stone: Best Friends Forever!* to Rosalba as a gesture of gratitude for her friendship. The original *Stick and Stone* was written by Beth Ferry and illustrated by Tom Lichtenheld in 2015. It has brought me joy and laughter while inspiring reflections on friendships. This book is about friends who stick up for each other. At the start of the story, Stick and Stone are lonely and alone. When Stick sticks up for Stone after Pinecone bullies Stone, a friendship is born. No longer alone, they wander and explore until a loud hurricane threatens their activities, but once again, these friends are there for each other.

Beth Ferry explained that the first Stick and Stone book was about how one friend was brave enough to stick up for the other friend. The adventures that the characters have are reminiscent of what friends do together. When Ferry wrote the new book, she recognized that Stick and Stone had been friends for six years, which was long enough for friends to feel like family (Schulze 2021).

Reading *Stick and Stone*
Photo Credit: Diane Kashin

My love for this book has solidified as I have watched my grandchildren fall in love with it too. In the follow-up book, Stone supports Stick in his search for his family tree. They wander through forests galore. Will Stick ever find where he lived before his branch broke? After getting lost during their quest, a rehabilitated Pinecone comes to their rescue! "Stick, Stone, no longer alone. Stick, Stone, saved by Pinecone!" In the end, Stick recognizes that he will never find his family tree but realizes, with Stone's help, that friends are family.

Ferry explains that she often asks children about whether Stick and Stone should forgive Pinecone for being a bully. She says that it isn't easy to forgive someone for hurting your feelings, but it is important. By giving

Pinecone the opportunity to help Stick and Stone, even though they are not great friends, the author demonstrates that you can be unkind but can also redeem yourself. This book about friendship is also about forgiveness. I think about my professional friends when I reflect on this book.

1 Should Stick and Stone expand their duo into a trio of friends to include Pinecone?
2 How important is it for professional friendship duos to engage with other professional friends?
3 If a professional friend or colleague has hurt your feelings, should you forgive them?

I have not spoken to my former friend since our friendship ended, and it has taken years for me to forgive them. The burden of sadness and anger was heavy. According to the American Psychological Association Dictionary of Psychology, forgiveness, like friendship, is voluntary. We must deliberately change our feelings toward someone we believe has caused hurt or harm. Letting go of negative emotions means those emotions no longer take up space in my heart. I hope that my former friend has forgiven me. My heart is lighter and now more open for my professional friends, some of whom, like Rosalba, have become like family.

Four Questions for My Friend: Rosalba

1 **After reading the chapter, what sparked your interest?**

I am sparked by the concepts of voice and image. As I read this section, I recalled the times that I had doubted myself. My feelings of uncertainty rendered me speechless so that I couldn't find the words to describe the thoughts and ideas in my head. Trying to speak of what I already know is difficult at times. Perhaps I am afraid of expressing myself, but I do value others and their voices. When I first met Diane, I felt I was being heard for the very first time. It wasn't and still isn't easy. It continues to be a challenge to describe my thoughts in words. I am left wondering about the connection between voice and image as I continue to reflect on the value of professional friends as confidants. When your friend whom you trust is your sounding board, your voice can be heard.

2 **As you considered this spark/interest, how has your thinking moved with it?**

Reflecting on voice, my thinking is moving in the direction of the pedagogy of listening and relationships. I get very excited when I listen to others speak of passions and dreams that are similar to mine, and I want to shout out my thoughts and excitement. Sometimes I feel blocked with this excitement and find that I am not listening as well as I could be. Then I refocus myself to become that better listener. I am a very good observer. Sometimes I think I can sense the character of another during a first encounter. Sometimes this impacts my conversations and my ability to listen. I'm working on it. I do think it's important for us to give voice to each other, as it is a way of valuing each other, building on mutual respect, trust, and care. I am thinking about how our profession can move more toward the heart of teaching and learning. I am often pulled to the words of Loris Malaguzzi about identity, schools as places of identity, adults and children in relationships, and relationships that are deep, meaningful, and caring.

3 **After considering questions one and two, what connections are you making to your own experiences with professional friends?**

I have had so many discussions with Diane over the years about early childhood education in relationship to our community. We struggle with this at times, and I feel a little frustrated and confused. Recently, Diane has me thinking about how we can move forward and follow our dreams while not thinking about what others think. Not worrying about what others think about you is something I really need to continue to work on, because it is out of my control and really none of my business. I don't need everyone to like me or listen to what I have to say, but I value respect. I am uncomfortable and uneasy navigating professional relationships when I don't feel there is mutual respect. For many years, I was a volunteer board member for an organization that promoted the Reggio Emilia approach, but it did not model the philosophy. I tried to voice my concerns but felt discouraged when I was questioned in a diminishing way. I resigned and was very distraught as it was not a place where voice and relationships were supported. It was a toxic environment. It was a very difficult decision. I am grateful to my friends, including Diane, who supported me during this challenging time.

4 **What advice can you give to the readers of this book to help them on their journeys with professional friends?**

My advice is to definitely find a professional friend who will lift your spirits but challenge you to higher levels. Your friend can provoke your thinking and creativity and give you the courage to find joy in your work. I think it is important to have this kind of friendship because it gives you the good, and it gives you a little bit of everything in between so that you can grow to appreciate and love yourself. I want to be challenged because it makes me read, think, listen, and observe more. I am forever filled with gratitude for my professional friendships as they hold a very strong place in my life, and many friends have become like family to me.

—Rosalba Bortolotti

Chapter Three

Forging Friendships

REACHING THE SPIRIT

Hello, Friend!

When you bring to mind your professional friends, who do you see? Are most of your friends very similar to you, or do you see differences between yourself and your friends? A large body of research suggests that we have a preference for similarity when choosing friends. Do we choose friends who look like us, even though similar is not always better? Do you have a diverse friendscape, and are you grateful for what these relationships bring to your life? This chapter celebrates diversity in professional friendships. It speaks to the spirit and the importance of kindness and reciprocity. It is through a diverse friendship base that I have been able to forge a friendship characterized by kindness that has reached the spiritual realm.

When our friends represent diverse religions, races, sexual orientations, ages, backgrounds, and other characteristics, we benefit, especially when our friends are kind. Angela Bahns is a social psychologist who does research on prejudice, diversity beliefs, and friendship formation. According to Bahns (2019), the advantages of such friendships for adults and children are widely reported, and they include a reduction of prejudice and an increased openness to others.

Psychologist Gwendolyn Seidman (2018) examined research about why we tend to prefer people who are similar to us and found a connection to perception. *Perception* means becoming aware through the senses to attain understanding. To perceive, we interpret or look at someone or something in a particular way. You can only know your friends through your perceptions of them. Perceptions become memories that stay with you beyond the moment in which an action happened. Perceptions are also shaped by personality and temperament, and by our own pasts. The research findings indicate that in long-term situations—in which people have more of a chance to really know each other, like in long-term friendships or romantic relationships—*actual* similarity has less of an effect on whether a connection forms than *perceived* similarity does. This is in part because we have already filtered out dissimilar people with whom we have nothing in common.

Thinking Back

Patti Miller (2022) has written a memoir that tells the story of the nature of her friendships, featuring one friend who left her bereft and devasted by deciding to end the relationship for unexplained reasons. My own perceptions of past friendships are influenced by my brain's ability to remember. It is hard to write a memoir without memory. Researchers Thanujeni Pathman and Patricia Bauer write in the *Encyclopedia on Early Childhood Development* (2020) that our memories form the basis for our senses of self, guide our thoughts and decisions, influence our emotional reactions, and allow us to learn.

Our memory is divided into three parts: (1) sensory memory that gathers information through the senses in the moment and lasts less than a second, (2) short-term memory that gathers information about what happened and lasts thirty seconds to two minutes, and (3) long-term memory that is stored in specific sites around the brain and can last a lifetime. It represents the translation of the experiences from the physical to the representational (Miller 2022).

I was diagnosed with breast cancer early in 2019. Surgery, chemotherapy, and radiation treatments followed. I have been dealing with what is called "chemo brain" or cancer-related cognitive change since. It has been a long struggle. Writing has helped preserve my memory. Having memory loss is challenging, yet in some ways helpful when the memories are difficult. During the many months that I endured the treatments, hair loss, fatigue, and sickness, I remember the friends who were there for me and those who were not. I have lost my memories of the descriptive details, but the feelings and names endure. Erica, who is younger than my youngest child, texted me almost daily just to see how I was doing. Regardless of our age difference, we share similar passions about playing and learning. I know that Erica perceives me as a mentor, but I do pass power! I have learned from Erica, and she supported me during the time of COVID when I pivoted from workshops to webinars. I feel her support, and I benefited from her knowledge and skills. Erica is a true friend even though we are dissimilar in age.

It takes time to forge a friendship. A study by researcher Jeffrey Hall (2019), published by the *Journal of Social and Personal Relationships*, suggests that to become close friends, you need two hundred hours or more together. It is at our work environments that we can find that amount of time! Indeed, you may lack the time needed to know someone outside of the work environment. Because making friends is linked to many benefits, including overall well-being and a reduction in one's risk of dying, turning to your work context to cultivate friendships might be a good idea. If these friendships reflect diversity, they also expand our professional horizons and support our development.

Think about diversity in professional friendships and how your friendships have formed. How do you establish a friendship, and how you do you maintain it? Think about the rapport that you have with your professional friends. *Rapport* is a friendly, harmonious relationship characterized by agreement, mutual understanding, or empathy that makes communication possible or easy.

1. In what ways do your professional friendships reflect diversity, and how would you describe your differences?
2. How would you describe the similarities between you and your professional friends?
3. What have you learned from your professional friendships that reflects a perspective that you did not previously know or understand?
4. What benefits have you gained from being in a professional friendship?
5. What do you understand about your friend's feelings?
6. Would you describe the communication in your dyad as easy?
7. Do you have disagreements or dissent with your professional friends?
8. How do you solve conflicts?

Parallels between Children and Adults

The search for friendship is part of children's lives from infancy. Dennie Palmer Wolf (2004), a leading researcher on early childhood development, suggests that relationships should be part of the curriculum, alongside science, technology, arts, and math. Likewise, the search for friendships and the need to understand relationships should be part of professional learning and viewed in parallel with children, families, and teachers. It is a multilayered approach like a complex spiderweb.

The threads of a web are interconnected, beginning at the center and moving outward. Think about how a spider spins its web. Such power from a small wonder of nature! Let's take some inspiration from this eight-legged spinner of silk. It is no surprise that the spider has inspired many Indigenous stories. Grandmother Spider is the weaver of dreams, planter of gardens, and spinner of webs. She aids others with her wisdom. Some Muskogee elders make dream catchers, which resemble a spiderweb, for children so that good fortune will come their way. In some Ojibwe stories, dream catchers are attributed to the Spider Woman, a spiritual protector of the young (Max 2007). Early childhood educators are protectors of the young even as they weave a world of wonders. They help children see and feel the threads that connect us all, so while nurturing learning they build relationships in wondrous ways.

You have the competence to view professional friendships from multiple and diverse perspectives. To reach a critical level of reflection, being open to diversity is necessary. To understand the perspectives of others, we must expand our relationships to involve others who are different from us, and we must work on these friendships because they may not happen naturally. Friendships require thought and reflection about our friendship choices.

As early childhood educators, we see children's friendships form before our eyes on a daily basis. How do we know whether these relationships should or will endure? How do we know when a friend is true? Reflecting on friendship formation between children, while thinking about how our own professional friendships form, is an example of a parallel process at play. Early childhood education expert Jane Bertrand (2017) speaks to the power of friendships in early childhood education, suggesting that children's peer-to-peer relationships are often overlooked by teachers. In what ways could teachers nurture and support peer-to-peer interactions? How can observations of these interactions inform the invitations for play that are offered to children?

Wolf (2004) suggests going beyond a surface view of friendships. Think about these basic skills of friendship formation and then take your reflections to a higher and deeper level. As you read the bullet points, think first about children, then reflect on your own friendships. A friend is

- able to approach others
- able to be interesting
- able to get along
- able to negotiate conflict

Coming to the Edge of the Circle

I love my family and friends. But not everything I love is animate. I love nesting dolls, vintage buttons, and natural loose parts like beach glass, tree cookies, and acorns. I love blocks of all shapes and sizes. I also love ideas, concepts, and reflections. Spiritual connections can feel bodiless, ethereal, and formless. My friend Hopi calls it the "Great Kind Mystery" (Martin 2021, 143). Hopi inspires me to be kind. I want to care, to be kind, to be available, and to pay attention to the sources of my love. I am inspired by others who embody these ways of being. Hopi is kind. He signs his emails with "In kindness." When I met Hopi, I felt he was approachable, so I reached out after our initial meeting. I wanted to learn from him, and what I have learned is the importance of kindness, respect, and reciprocity. I am not sure why I felt compelled to reach out, given that we were so different. It is a wonderful mystery.

Featured Friend: Hopi

I met Hopi when we were asked to co-present a webinar. This was a few years before webinars became commonplace. During a trial run, I couldn't get my new microphone to work! It was embarrassing. In a respectful and kind way, Hopi helped me figure out the problem. The webinar went much better than I thought it would, and it felt wonderful—even empowering—to have been a recipient of kindness and respect. This experience stayed with me, and months later I thought of Hopi after I had been gently and lovingly challenged by friends to include an Indigenous perspective in a five-day outdoor professional event that I was planning. I am grateful I reached out to Hopi and grateful for how our relationship has enriched and informed my worldview. As I navigate the final season of my professional life, it is from Hopi that I have begun to shape my legacy. I am beyond grateful. From Hopi I have learned to embrace my identity, which includes who I am and where I come from. From this base, I can now be open to new experiences that help me see beyond my own perspective. I have a fuller view of early childhood education and a deeper understanding of what the next generation needs from me. I learned from Hopi's teachings while in relationship with my friend. He has been my mentor, but he has been open to learning more about early childhood education from me. We have a reciprocal relationship of professional friendship. We walk together on the land with early childhood educators, teaching and learning with children in mind, heart, and spirit.

In this chapter, I tell my story about the Hopi and Diane dyad. I am overwhelmingly grateful for my friendship with Hopi and offer the greatest and biggest expression of thanks, *G'ichi Miigwech*.

In my friendship with Hopi, I continue to learn about the sacred protocol that Gokoomis Jacque refers to as *Asemaa Nitam* ("tobacco first"). From her teachings, Hopi has embraced this discipline so that each endeavor on his life path is done in a good way. Hopi shares his perspective about the traditional tobacco protocol on the Edge of the Bush website (edgeofthebush.ca). He describes it as a way of beginning and walking with kindness throughout our interactions and particularly across cultures. The English word *protocol* indicates a level of respect for these nation-to-nation interactions that are needed between Indigenous and settler nations (Martin 2021).

From Hopi, I learned that this most sacred medicine is a medicine of kindness. It connects back to an Anishinaabe creation story in which *Asemaa* is given as an act of kindness and reciprocity before asking or taking anything. Wrapping *Asemaa* in cloth and ribbon, you offer it like a present. You speak about yourself and your intentions, and then you make your request. You give before taking. When I prepared my offering to Hopi and asked him to join me on this friendship journey, I wrapped the tobacco in a fabric napkin given to me by my husband's grandmother, Bubbie Dorothy. This family heirloom is a tribute to her love and kindness. It was given in that spirit.

Hopi and Diane

Photo Credit: Rosalba Bortolotti

I am grateful that Hopi accepted the offering. He did have the freedom to refuse it, but I think he knew he could help me in my research on professional friends. According to Hopi, not every tribe, nation, or Indigenous community follows *Asemaa Nitam*. Elders and teachers from different nations follow different ways. However, it is very common among many (if not all) Indigenous nations around the world to have some form of protocol that begins a relationship with reciprocity and respect (Martin n.d.).

The Offering

Photo Credit: Diane Kashin

Hopi's research is grounded in the methodology of the Ojibwe Sacred Circle. I can only come to the edge of this circle and share my perceptions with you. It is through my relationship with Hopi and his auntie that I am able to do this. While I am only beginning to learn a little bit about that Ojibwe methodology, I have found that the circle teachings of the Seasonal Pedagogy have helped me frame my reflections on professional friendships.

Circles symbolize openness, peace, and comfort. I believe that symbols are brought into our lives to awaken our souls, offer lessons, and help us heal. An article written by Jean Stevenson (1999) in the *Native Social Work Journal* describes the healing aspects of a circle from an Indigenous perspective. The circle is a sacred symbol and key to spirituality. It is symbolic of the cycle of life and of all things being interrelated. It acknowledges that when we share pain, laughter, and love, it brings us closer together. We can learn from each other's experiences. Being part of a circle can have a profound impact on our beings.

I have personally experienced the healing power of a sharing circle, as it offers opportunities to share, learn, trust, care, and support others. I am grateful for these experiences and to the circle symbol for the energy it affords us to be critically reflective. The circle has an openness to it, something that can bring peace and comfort. It's cyclical, encapsulating new beginnings, connecting with seasonal and lunar transitions. Even the planets, chakras (energy points in one's body), and our breath cycle are circular. In a circle, everything is equal, balanced, and interconnected. We are all part of the circle that is Mother Earth.

The circle has practical and historical meaning in early childhood education. From a Western, Eurocentric perspective, *circle time* as it exists today originated from Friedrich Froebel's kindergarten pedagogy. He believed that being in a circle formation represented a connection to our soul and spirit. When I have been part of sacred circles with Hopi, no one sits before, behind, or below us. We keep a space open facing east that invites the spirits and our ancestors into this sacred circular space.

Applying the Seasonal Pedagogy to Play

In his PhD thesis, Hopi explains that it was during observations of his own children's "extended unstructured play times close to Mother Earth" that he could see "a circular pattern to their play that followed a natural cycle." This perspective of play did not connect with any of his "Western education teacher training" (Martin 2021, x). There are many possible applications for this natural and dynamic framework grounded in gratitude and love for Mother Earth, the ultimate early childhood educator. These questions are a frame for reflections on children's play and learning as well as the play and learning we do with our professional friends. Figure 3.1 invites you to read the questions from the bottom up to reflect in a naturally circular way about what can be sparked by unstructured play.

You will see that just as this cycle happens naturally in children's play and learning, it also happens naturally in professional learning. It can be applied to pedagogical documentation and to the curriculum path going forward. It supports a process of critical reflection that leads to meaning making.

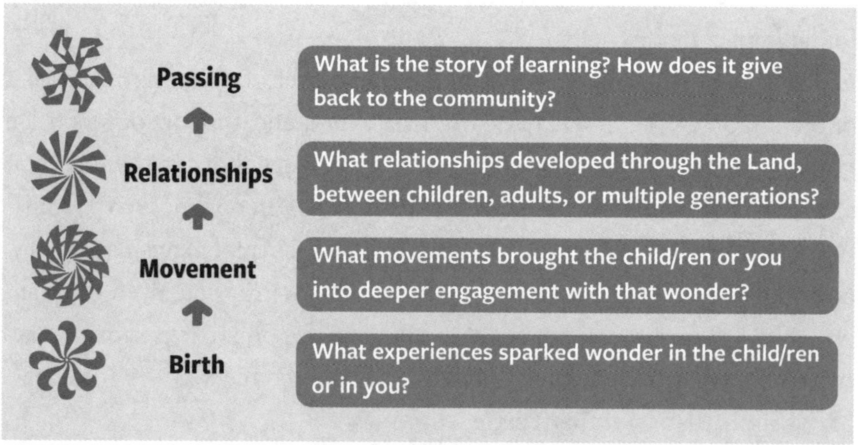

Figure 3.1 Mother Earth Guides Play and Learning

When I look at my life and apply the seasonal cycle, I see that I am in the season connected to passing. I am ready to share my stories of professional friendships. This photo of my grandson, entering a *Wiigiwaam* ("bush shelter"/"home") that he and I helped construct alongside Hopi and others from local Indigenous communities, is the embodiment of the circle of life. My grandson is entering the world, and it is my role to support his connection to Mother Earth throughout the time we have together. We have an intergenerational relationship grounded by shared experiences in nature. This is something I learned from Hopi that I am passing on to Griffen.

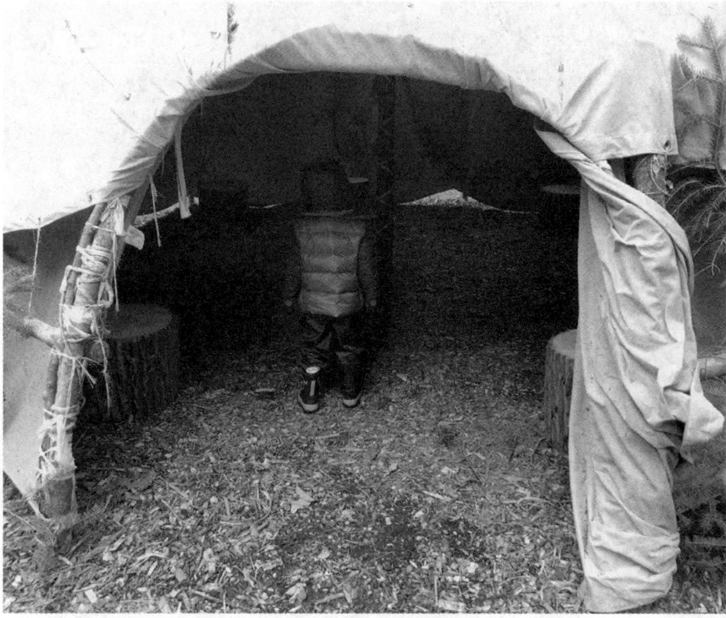

Griffen at Nature School

Photo Credit: Diane Kashin

Learning is about relationships to each other, the materials, and the land. Pedagogical documentation is about sharing stories of these relationships to make the learning visible. One of the first ways I applied the Seasonal Pedagogy was to see it through the lens of documentation. I visit a local pond seasonally with Griffen. It is filled with frogs, insects, birds, cattails, and more. The pond is our teacher. Our pond experiences were documented with four photos over four seasons and are featured in figure 3.2.

Our experience at the pond began in the spring, the season of new beginnings. This is when the natural world revives and reinvigorates after the colder winter months. Plants begin to grow again, with new seedlings sprouting and animals waking from hibernation. As we moved into the summer, the warmest season of the year when everything is lush and green, Griffen became fascinated with the cattails. He picked one up from the ground and talked about the texture being smooth, furry, and soft. He opened the cattail to explore the fluff inside. I had expected him to want to bring it home, but he walked back to the edge of the pond and returned it to where he found it. He gave it back to Mother Earth. Later he asked about the fluff inside and what it was.

Figure 3.2 Documenting Four Seasons at the Pond

We continued to move together with this shared interest throughout the summer. As co-learners, we researched to learn that cattails are found worldwide. We then planted seeds and read stories about seeds. In the fall, when the leaves were on the ground and the geese were flying south, the cattails became brittle. This was the season when I realized that my time with Griffen had strengthened our relationship to the pond and to each other.

During the winter, when the days are short and the temperatures are cold, all that remained of the cattails was fluff. As the pond was blanketed by snow, it was time to think deeply about how our experiences could relate to the Seasonal Pedagogy. It was time to tell the story and create documentation. I am grateful to Hopi for this perspective as it helped me to understand the importance of finding the meaning in our stories.

Power, Language, and Relationships

Relationships are the key to life. What I have learned from professional friends is important, but it is the relationships themselves that are the most meaningful. Our friends give us connection. To take this gift and maintain our friendships, we need to give back. Professional friendships are reciprocal relationships of give-and-take.

When I met Hopi, I had just retired, but I wasn't ready to stop working in this new season of my life. I enjoy co-learning with others with aligning values. I wanted working relationships that were grounded in love, respect, and kindness. I no longer wanted to work in a context characterized by power differences and constant conflict or in a way that was not representative of a parallel process of learning. I no longer wanted to seek power.

The giving of power is a good way to lead one's life. Hopi describes the Ojibwe teachings of *Mino Bimaadiziwin* ("good life way") as the lived practice of the "four great principles of kindness, honesty, sharing, and strength" (Martin 2021, xv). I am motivated by my friend, for he shows me that it is possible to lead one's life in this way. This holistic, Earth-based approach now informs my pedagogical identity. I no longer want to think in a linear, compartmentalized way that feels separate from the Earth. In the spirit of giving back, I continue to share Hopi's work far and wide among all my relations because I believe in its possibilities to empower.

> *One who finds a faithful friend, finds a treasure.*
> ~ The Apocrypha (Sirach 6:14)

As a consequence of memory lapse and a lack of linguistic skill, I struggle to say some words regardless of language. I know from experiences with Hopi that it is not *how* you say the words to acknowledge others but that you try to say them. Words empower when they are spoken. That is the oral tradition. As I experienced passing the feather and putting tobacco on the fire while being present and listening to others try to pronounce the Ojibwe words, I understood how these words empower when spoken. The language Hopi shared was unfamiliar to those of us who were newly arrived in Canada as well as those whose ancestors arrived in the 1700s, but we all tried to say *miigwech* ("thanks") or use *Nanaboozhoo* (greetings in the name of the Ojibwe First Teacher). Perhaps we sensed Hopi's kindness and wanted to give back in kind.

Speaking the words, even if the pronunciation is not accurate, shows the good intentions of the speaker. I learned from my daughter to accept prayers, greetings, kind thoughts, and gestures in any denomination or language. Using the language of another to express good thoughts is quite powerful. I felt it myself when my new grandson was born. I was excited to hold Wesley for the first time and share my good news on social media. I valued all the kind expressions offered but really appreciated when my friends said *mazel tov*, a Jewish phrase expressing congratulations or wishing someone good luck. This is the language of my ancestors, and it reflects my identity. It is a kind gesture of friendship that connects to the spiritual domain.

Spiritual Perspectives

I have been deeply influenced by the perspectives from Reggio Emilia, Italy, and the Indigenous teachings shared by Hopi. I am grateful to a new friend, Deborah Schein, for helping me connect to my own cultural identity as she kindly shared perspectives grounded in the teachings of Judaism. As we learn from the Jewish philosopher Emil Fackenheim (1916–2003), seeing other perspectives is not to vindicate one or the other as superior or unique

Introducing Wesley Myles Kashin

Photo Credit: Ben Kashin

(Schein and Schein n.d.). Rather, professional friends with diverse perspectives will appreciate commonalities and recognize each other's strengths.

When we are open to spiritual perspectives, our reflections deepen. Spirituality reflects "deep connections and moments of wonder rather than a focus on God and religion" (Schein 2017, 2). In *Belonging, Being, and Becoming: The Early Years Learning Framework for Australia*, spiritual development is defined as "a range of human experiences including a sense of awe and wonder, and an exploration of being and knowing" (Council of Australian Governments 2009, 49). Freya Lucas (2019) writes in *The Sector*, an early childhood education newsletter also from Australia, that focusing a lens on spiritual development is helpful in a complex, diverse, and sometimes unkind world.

Relationships are fundamental to our spiritual needs. Friendships in particular make our lives manageable and fulfilling emotionally, spiritually, and psychologically. When we cultivate these relationships, we are better able to cope with the stresses and challenges of life. Children need spiritually healthy teachers.

In her work on spiritual development in children, Deborah provides a lens from which to examine our own spiritual development in a parallel process of reflection. Her definition of spiritual development is ever evolving. Spirituality is "as complex and invisible to the naked eye as intellectual development, as deep-seated as emotional development, and as integrative as social development." In fact, Deborah's research "shows that spiritual development" may be "the precursor to all other areas of development" (Schein 2017, 8). Spiritual development as a range of human experiences includes love, relationships, a positive sense of self, acts of caring, kindness, empathy, awe, wonder, joy, and inner peace. We can see how nurturing these dispositions in children and in ourselves will support our developing friendships and so much more.

- Wonder and wonderment: *Wonder*, the noun, is defined as feelings of surprise mixed with admiration "stimulated by beauty, the unexpected, or the unfamiliar." *Wonder*, the verb, refers to the desire or curiosity to know something that leads to pondering big questions. *Wonderment* "reflects feelings of surprise or amazement when something out of the ordinary occurs" (Schein 2017, 79–80).
- Awe: As a noun or a verb, *awe* refers to "feelings of respect and wonder sometimes mixed with a little fear" (Schein 2017, 80).

- Joy: Most often associated with happiness, *joy* involves basic needs such as our need for friendship but can also be achieved by "learning a skill, solving a problem, or exposing our complex dispositions of caring, kindness, empathy and reverence to the world" (Schein 2017, 80).

Deborah suggests that spiritual development can be nurtured in and with nature. Spend time in nature with children, by yourself, and with your friends as a means of developing the whole self.

Making Connections to Pedagogical Practice: Spiritual Moments

Deborah identified five different types of spiritual moments that can take individuals beyond themselves, including moments in time, in space, with nature, in strong relationships, and with big questions. Spiritual moments in time refers to children's need to have calm and quiet times every day as well as extended time to play. This is a time for children to "meander and explore inner thoughts and dive into self-chosen experiences," a fruitful time to learn about a "child's inner thoughts [and] images of self" through observation (Schein 2017, 99). As a provoking proposal, I offer you an invitation to observe one child or a small group of children during these spiritual moments in time.

Provoking Proposal: During a morning or afternoon, take multiple photos of a child or children as they are engaged in meandering and exploring in and with nature. Review these photos and choose four that will tell the story of the moment in time. Think deeply and critically about this experience. Did the photo taking keep you from being in the moment with the children?

Utilizing the Seasonal Pedagogy and the What? Then What? So What? Now What? framework that is featured below, what can you learn about children's spiritual development? What can you learn about your practice of observation and documentation?

What? Then What? So What? Now What?

What? So What? Now What? (W3) is a framework or pedagogical approach that helps adult learners reflect on a shared experience to identify ways to improve or act. Researched and developed by Gary Rolfe, Dawn Freshwater, and Melanie Jasper (2001), it is also attributed to Henri Lipmanowicz and Keith McCandless (2013), who identified it as a liberating structure. Liberating structures are frameworks that help us work, lead, and co-create

(Razzetti 2019). The power of liberating structures is that they are easy to remember and comprehend.

As I collaborated with Hopi, we took the three pronged framework and added *Then What?* to make a connection to the Seasonal Pedagogy. I have applied this W4 structure to reflections on pedagogical documentation and observations of children's play. I offer it now as a means to reflect on shared experiences with professional friends. Table 3.1 demonstrates how this liberating structure can be applied. Imagine using the W4 framework after observing a professional friend facilitate a play experience with young children. It will give you a moment for reflection before you respond with helpful and supportive feedback. Use W4 to reflect on professional learning and to demonstrate and document professional growth.

What? *Birth*	This is an objective question.	Describe what you saw and heard. What led to the beginning of the shared experience?
Then What? *Movement*	This is a reflection question.	Reflect on how the shared experience evolved. How did those involved move with experience?
So What? *Relationships*	This is an interpretation question.	What was meaningful about the experience? What learning occurred? What relationships were formed?
Now What? *Passing*	This is a decision question.	Where will you go next? How does the experience inform your practice? How can you apply the new knowledge/understanding to your practice? What is the story of the learning? How will you tell it?

Table 3.1 Reflection and a Seasonal Pedagogy

Big Ideas of Professional Friendships: Reciprocity

Trust leads to a relationship of reliance and reciprocity. We don't want friendships that are lopsided with one or the other friend feeling like they are always giving. Support should flow both ways. It should be reciprocal. *Reciprocity* is a situation in which parties agree to help each other by behaving in the same way or giving each other similar advantages. Friendships are reciprocal because they are characterized by mutual dependence and influence.

Reciprocity is often associated with Indigenous people. In Canada and many other parts of the world, Indigenous perspectives have been ignored and marginalized through a process of colonization, even after signing internationally recognized treaties. The Truth and Reconciliation Commission of Canada focused on establishing and maintaining a mutually respectful relationship between Indigenous and non-Indigenous peoples in ways that demonstrated reciprocity. While taking individual paths toward truth and reconciliation in our lives and practices, we can also consider how reciprocity influences professional friendships and children's experiences with Mother Earth. Hopi sees reciprocity as a way of being on the land with children. The "simple act of recognizing that children need to touch Mother Earth and be given the freedom to discover and explore their natural curiosities can be seen as an act of reciprocity" (Martin 2021, 90).

The act of reciprocity is significant in establishing and maintaining relationships. The give-and-take of professional friendships may not always feel reciprocal when friends are not responsive to each other. Listening to our friends requires learning about them.

Names and Knowing Each Other

We learn from our professional friends when we listen to their stories about their names. Our names are an integral part of our identities, but they can also be a springboard for making assumptions about each other. Michael Hedrik (2015), in an article from *The Week*, suggests that when a new person introduces themselves to you, your first instinct is to assemble a rough mental sketch of everyone you have ever known with that name. You may subsequently judge or stereotype this person subconsciously based on other people with the same name.

Hopi describes his dissertation journey as needing to begin by learning about himself, including his family history and where he comes from. In his journey to learn about himself, guided by Gokoomis Jacque, he searched for the meaning of his names given at birth. He shares this with others who sit in the circle with him. He tells us who he is, the land that knows him, where he comes from, and what is in his heart. From these shared experiences that

I have had with Hopi, I see the importance of our names and how sharing their meanings can be a catalyst for getting to know our friends.

I am Diane Kashin, née Lackman, which I have understood as meaning "man of the lake." I was given the Hebrew name Dina when I was born on lands of the Kanien'kehá:ka Nation, known as Montreal and historically a gathering place for many First Nations. I am the daughter of Reeva Feinberg. My mother came to Canada from eastern Europe when she was three months old with her mother, Dina. Dina was born in 1890 in Kishinev, Moldavia, the eldest of four sisters. In 1923 she met and married my grandfather, Haim, who came from Kyiv, Ukraine. *Haim* in Hebrew means "life." My grandfather immigrated to Canada shortly after, not knowing that my grandmother was pregnant. In 1924 Dina left from Odessa to join my grandfather with one of her sisters and my mother. The photo below pictures my grandmother and mother when they arrived in Montreal.

I don't know much about the family of my father, Gerald. His father had died tragically when he was quite young, and he didn't have a good relationship with his mother, Molly, whom I loved dearly. My father was brilliant but extremely troubled. An engineer by trade, his passions spanned from science to literature to history to religion. When my father felt well and I felt safe, the stories he spun could take you away to another time and place. He often told me the story of Molly's father, who had settled in Canada in the late 1800s. My father told tales of his grandfather trading with both the

Dina and Reeva, circa 1924

Photo Credit: Unknown

Indigenous people and French colonists. According to family lore, he came to be known as *le bon Juif*, or "the good Jew," because of his kindness and good relationships.

When I was seven, we moved to Toronto, and many of my enduring friendships were born. It is where I met my best friend, my husband, Lorne. Together we raised three children and now have three grandchildren.

I acknowledge and I am thankful for all the Indigenous people who cared for the land and continue to care for the land on which my children and grandchildren play and learn. I am also thankful to you, reader. Thank you for listening to my family stories. What do you think would be the impact of sharing your family stories with your professional friends? Would it help you move beyond judgments to increased understanding and trust? Share the stories of who you are with your friends. To be a true friend, we need to take the time to do this.

1. Who are you?
2. What is the meaning of your name?
3. Where do you come from?
4. What land knows you?
5. What are your traditions?
6. What are some words used to describe your traditions?
7. What is moving in your mind about professional friendships?
8. What do you feel in your heart about professional friendships?

In my heart, I feel love for my professional friends. It is through the heart and spirit that I have been able to put aside my imposter syndrome to forge friendships that feel good. These friendships offer me support and encouragement. My friends challenge and provoke me from a basis of trust, love, and kindness. It is through my professional friends that I have been able to heal emotionally and physically.

It is because of the kindness of my friends that I have been able to see beyond self and to recognize that I can be open to the perspectives of others. It was Hopi who helped me envision a different way to approach the practice of pop-up adventure playgroups. Prior to meeting Hopi, I had spent a few years organizing and facilitating these experiences. He helped me recognize that while bringing pool noodles and cardboard tubes to the forest might provide a fun afternoon, it was obscuring what is meaningful about children's interactions with the invitations of Mother Earth. I wrote the following scenario to remind me about the importance of kindness and diversity in perspectives. I hope it resonates with you.

In Your Mind's Eye

Imagine that you have attended an early childhood education conference with your professional friend and room partner. You go to different workshops but meet over lunch. Your friend is very excited to show you photos from the pop-up adventure playground she attended. As you swipe through the photos, you see a beautiful forest full of junk. You begin to judge your friend in your mind because when you see the forest, you see potential in what the land itself has to offer and question what you are seeing in the photos. You recognize that you are shifting away from your friend but still wish to hear their enthusiasm and excitement. Before you head back to your hotel room, you suggest that you and your friend continue walking and talking in the forest so you can connect to Mother Earth without tires, fabric, tubes, hoses, bales, and industrial spools.

When you listen to your friend, giving them space to talk without interruption and hearing their voice, you decenter yourself. Decentering means you become open to multiple and diverse perspectives and become fully present for the other person. Have the confidence to know that you don't have to respond and deflect to your own experiences and perspectives. If you avoid this shifting response and remain focused on your friend, you will be able to reply with love in a way that will be empowering. Know that you will be walking together with your friend. You will learn together what Mother Earth can teach you both. It is a good beginning.

Invitations from Mother Earth

An invitation is the act of inviting or presenting a situation in a manner that elicits curiosity. I believe that everything we do with children should be invitational, to support the premise that children learn through play. Play is freely chosen. When children have access to unstructured play, they have control over the play activity. Children's sense of agency is fostered through self-directed play, and self-directed play inspires rich learning. An invitation can plant a seed, ready to sprout. Mother Earth provides invitations every day across the four seasons. They happen naturally during free play on the land. You cannot predetermine outcomes, as every day brings something new that can spark children's interests.

One spring day, on the way to the pond, Griffen stopped to examine the many worms scattered on the path. We had never seen so many worms before. Some were moving, and some were not. Mother Earth had offered an invitation. Griffen responded and was provoked to engage. When we returned from our adventure, we had deeper conversations about seasons, life, and death. Griffen formed a relationship with the squiggly creatures. Our intergenerational relationship grew stronger as we shared in the continuing saga of Griffen and his bubbie.

If a child chooses to interact with Mother Earth's offerings, the invitation is accepted and the child engages. This spark evokes a response, and it is then that you have a provocation. *Provocation* is a complicated term as it can mean so much. Educators, according to Susan Fraser (2000), provoke children to think more deeply or broadly about an invitation to learn. The provocation is a response that implies further action. If the invitation is ignored, it did not provoke, and you can take the opportunity to reflect on why. If the invitation is accepted and sprouts into a provocation, the possibilities for inquiry are endless.

Inquiry can also emerge through the sharing of stories. I read *The Scarecrow* by Beth Ferry (2019) to Griffen. The tender story unites the seemingly inanimate scarecrow with a random visitor, a baby crow. Even though all the other animals are afraid of the scarecrow, the small, vulnerable little crow becomes a friend. This is the story of an unlikely but true and diverse friendship that can weather the changing of the seasons. "He never rests. He never bends. He's never had a single friend, for all the woodland creatures know, not to mess with old Scarecrow." (p. 6) The story unfolds as the crow grows older and flies away. Once again, Scarecrow is alone, but then the crow returns with his mate and brings a whole nest of baby birds to Scarecrow.

Griffen was very touched by Scarecrow's kindness and the little baby bird. It reminded us of the story I had told him months before, which Hopi had told me. When you see crows, it is your aunties and grandmothers checking in on you. I will never forget when, months after hearing the story for the first time, Griffen opened the front door to a murder of crows and exclaimed, "Hello, Grandma Mina," naming his mother's beloved grandmother who passed a few months after he was born. This was a multigenerational spiritual experience that connected us to our ancestors. When I see crows, I feel the presence of my grandmothers, Molly, Dina, and Dorothy.

Thank You for Being a Friend

I don't remember much about the day that Hopi interviewed me for his thesis, but I am thankful for the experience. It was soon after my cancer treatments, during the COVID-19 pandemic, and it was wintery cold! Now when I read my words, I recognize it as the beginning of this journey of exploring professional friendships.

> I want to give back to those who I have connected with, to the people who are continuing to teach children while I am no longer in the classroom or on the land with kids. So, I think it is important, but I think it is also important because it is about voice, and it is about expression and sharing your wisdom. And that is something children can do. That is something educators can do. (Martin 2021, 111)

I am grateful to Hopi for sharing his perspectives. I am thankful that I have been open to receive them.

Four Questions for My Friend: Hopi

1. **After reading the chapter, what sparked your interest?**

   For me, the spark of inspiration comes from your interest to support your circle of professional friends in relationship to your experiences of the Sacred Circle with Dr. Gokoomis Jacque and I. Working between cultures and worldviews at the "edge of the bush" in an ethical and relational way continues to challenge our collective efforts at truth and reconciliation between Indigenous and settler folks here in Canada. Because of the history of colonization and the pervasive force of taking before giving, "establishing and maintaining respectful relationships" (TRC of Canada 2015, 6) between Indigenous peoples and settler folks is often thwarted in these cross-cultural contexts.

2. **As you considered this spark/interest, how has your thinking moved with it?**

   I have been so grateful for how you have respectfully adapted the Seasonal Pedagogy that I shared with you to reflect on this key issue of friendship in professional contexts. The colonized structures of power and hierarchy that many of us have grown up immersed in continue to thwart the professional friendships that have been so valuable to the progression of our work together.

3 **After considering questions one and two, what connections are you making to your own experiences with professional friends?**

As one of your professional friends, I appreciated being introduced to your wider circle of friends that includes such a range of cultures, experiences, and backgrounds. I was particularly grateful for your willingness to work with the Seasonal Pedagogy and make space for Indigenous knowledge in your circle of support for those professional friends. Grounding your work in this way was not only kind for the Anishinaabe educators you included, but it also offered a holistic experience of that kindness for all the people you involved. Since this experience, I am convinced that everyone needs their circle of support and that your concept of professional friends is key to supporting the creation of those contexts.

4 **What advice can you give to the readers of this book, to help them on their journeys with professional friends?**

Sustainable relationships require reciprocity and respect. Friends need to be equal partners in sustaining their relationship, which requires that each person take up their responsibilities, first to themselves, then to their family, before making relevant connections to the wider community. Those four *R*s (reciprocity, respect, relationships, and responsibilities) are well documented in Indigenous research contexts, but I believe they also apply to the ongoing sustenance of the circle of support that needs to be established and maintained between two people or a whole community. The ethical lessons of these principles are evident in every aspect of the natural world. Indigenous cultures all over the world have developed in relation to these principles of what some Ojibwe refer to as the Sacred Circle, so I would encourage readers to nurture professional friendships with a wide range of peoples and cultures. The circle can really be understood only from sharing and experiencing many diverse perspectives. What better way to come together as nations and peoples than in friendship!

—Dr. Hopi Martin

Chapter Four

Forging Friendships

ACTIVATING THE MIND

Hello, Friend!

> *Friendship is unnecessary, like philosophy, like art. . . . It has no survival value; rather it is one of those things which give value to survival* ~ C. S. Lewis, *The Four Loves*

High-quality early childhood classrooms provide children with many opportunities for inquiry-based explorations of the world so they can better understand and make meaning of it. Children constantly follow their curious minds, searching for answers to questions, seeking to make sense of the world around them, and exploring where they fit in a diverse social landscape. The themes of exploration, questioning, meaning, and identity have long been linked to the spiritual domain, yet the spiritual nature of childhood is often overlooked in mainstream early childhood settings. By examining how early childhood educators understand children's spirituality, we can explore new ways of thinking about holistic child development and the methods to enhance their play and learning.

Traditionally, early childhood education emphasizes the whole child, defined in four domains: intellectual, physical, emotional, and social. Many argue that these developmental domains should also include spirituality, as it has been overlooked in mainstream early childhood education (Mata-McMahon, Haslip, and Schein 2020). We can also take a holistic approach to professional friendships and focus on our whole beings: heart, spirit, and mind. You may connect with one friend through your heart and another via the spirit, and others may activate your mind.

This chapter is about true and lasting professional friendships that activate your mind and help you think about big ideas in early childhood education that have the potential to change your world. It is also about recognizing when friendships are over. Navigating the end of friendships challenges the heart, mind, and spirit. It can be a very troubling and tumultuous time, and I will be offering advice that I wish I had known, beginning with a reflection on what makes a true friend.

True and Lasting Friendships

For Aristotle, a Greek philosopher, a true friendship is not based on utility or pleasure but on mutual respect, admiration, and gratitude. A true friendship, a "friendship of the good," is different from the other types of friendships identified by philosophers (Petticrew 2018).

- *Friendships of utility* involve relationships where there is a transparent exchange of value.
- *Friendships of pleasure* involve friends with whom we enjoy being in the here and now.
- *Friendships of the good* are built on shared principles and virtues.

When I think of the first type of friendship, in my mind, I see Pat, my hairdresser. For the time we are together, we get along, converse, and laugh. I am grateful that I had a friend like Pat on my journey to regrow my hair, as I had many big feelings connected to this chemotherapy side effect. I trusted her with my vulnerability. Yet outside of hair appointments, we are not connected. You may have coworkers who represent a utility friendship. When you are together at work, you get along, but you aren't really close friends.

In the second level of friendship, you may not receive anything directly from your friend, but you do share enjoyment in some way. They are there with you, enjoying the same things you enjoy. You come together under that commonality. Pre-cancer and pre-pandemic, I used to take exercise classes at the community center. I made friends there, but our friendships did not endure. There were no conflicts or disagreements; the friendships ended because they were no longer part of my here-and-now activities.

Friendships of the good are what you want from a professional friend. This level of friendship represents the friends you have a deep connection with. Yet there is no assumption or obligation of having a good time. The friendships that last are those based on shared virtue and principles where conflicts are lovingly confronted.

When Friendships End

When my relationship with my former friend ended, my heart was heavy, and I missed our discussions. We could spend hours talking about practice and pedagogy. I learned so much from her. Meaningful and deep conversations would percolate in my head for days and days, nurturing my professional growth and learning. In the absence of these dialogues, I became fixated on trying to figure out what had led to the demise of our relationship. I now know that I missed the signals that our friendship was going awry.

When I look back, I can see now that the clues were there. We couldn't get past a disagreement. I complained constantly to my other friends, and it felt as if we were both just too busy for each other. Author Julia Dellitt (2022) provides these clues to when you may be outgrowing a friendship:

- You or your friend are "too busy" all the time. If you keep reaching out and you are not getting a return on your investment, think about whether you should continue investing in someone who doesn't prioritize you. If your friend is reaching out and you are coming up with excuses, then you are the one outgrowing the relationship.
- You don't really care to connect. Be honest with yourself and figure out why you're backing off. Do you even like this person? If a friendship no longer feels fun or fulfilling to you, don't pretend like it does.
- You crave new friendships. When you have outgrown a friendship and want to go in a different direction, ending one relationship opens up room for other, more positive connections. Tend to friendships that are worth keeping, but if you just have nothing in common anymore, leave those friendships and find better ones.
- The only thing you have in common is the past. Talking about positive past experiences with friends can be fun, but you need new memories too. Your friendships should support the present and future you. You may need to focus on friendships that can change with you instead of ones that hold you back in a certain place and time.
- You constantly complain about your friend. When a relationship is no longer working, you grumble relentlessly and steadily think or say a flood of snide remarks. You experience big feelings, and the negative emotions, whether annoyance, frustration, or stress, overtake more positive emotions.

- You can't get past a fight. Conflict can strengthen friendships if both parties are willing to communicate and work through an issue together. But sometimes it is difficult to bridge a divide, and you may not be able to work it out.
- You don't feel supported. Friends support each other, and they communicate what they need to feel supported. What's sufficient for one person may not be enough for another. It should still feel like a two-way street, where both friends try to show they care in a way that resonates with the other.
- You've run out of things to talk about. Some friendships simply dissipate, and the first sign is not having much to say to each other. If you are frustrated with small talk, it might be time to end the friendship.

I wish I had known about "the jar of pennies" when my friendship with my former friend was ending. If you put a penny into a jar each time a relationship makes you happy, but took a penny out each time it hurts you, how full would your jar be? If your jar is almost empty, meaning you feel hurt more than happy, the relationship isn't bringing value to your life. If the jar is fuller than you realize, the relationship might be worth saving. It might be time to forgive. Forgiving means accepting that someone did something that hurt you, trusting it won't happen again, and then completely moving on. Ask yourself these questions to decide whether you can forgive:

1. Imagine forgetting about the issue; would you be able to accept your friend for who they are?
2. Are you able to have a good, happy relationship again?
3. Is it just one specific problem, or multiple problems?
4. Can you make time for each other to work through the problem(s)?
5. Are you both willing to work toward solving the problem?
6. Does the solution end your complaints?
7. Is your friend willing to accept your forgiveness?
8. Is your friend willing to ask you for forgiveness?

If the complaining continues, perhaps the friendship needs to end. If it isn't just one issue but a pattern of more harm than happiness, perhaps it is time to cultivate more supportive relationships. I felt that with my former friend there were comparisons and envy. We were not each other's biggest cheerleader. The jealousy affected our friendship. Jealousy is a complex, big emotion that occurs when there is a real or perceived threat to a relationship.

If you think jealousy and competition have become part of your friendship, author Jacqueline DeMarco (2019) suggests that you try to intentionally focus on your friend's success. Your own success won't be delayed by helping a friend, but your friendship could crumble if you aren't supportive. I don't know whether this tactic would have helped our friendship at the time. I could have used the jealousy in our friendship as an opportunity to find out more about myself. Why was I sometimes jealous of her knowledge? Why did I feel competitive toward her? I felt that she was jealous of my accomplishments or else judging me for not being worthy of them. Had I recognized this as imposter syndrome, I might have been less envious and more supportive as a friend.

Author Paisley Gilmour (2021) suggests that we can cope with jealous feelings by shifting our thinking from being jealous to being grateful. My friend did offer different perspectives that expanded my knowledge, and I feel grateful for that. If I had focused on gratitude, I may have been able to overcome the jealousy more easily. I can accept that the relationship had to end. In the time of social media, however, experiencing the loss of a friend is difficult. You feel like you lost your best friend in front of the whole world. I was unfriended, blocked, and ghosted as my friend cut off all communication with me. There were no more texts or emails.

We can decide whether to have a difficult and blunt exchange that could hurt feelings or to ghost someone when a friendship goes awry. If you can have the conversation, be honest and kind, and then move on without burning bridges. The solution could be as simple as indicating that you don't currently have the extra capacity for a friendship. According to author Adam Popescu (2019), ghosting has to do with a person's comfort level with the status of the relationship and how they deal with their emotions. My friend reminded me in one of our last communications that she did not like confrontation and wanted to avoid it. As a friend, I could have thought of ways to make a reconciliation dialogue more comfortable, but I was so immersed in my own life stresses that I was unable to see beyond myself. I felt that I needed to go with what felt good and let go of what didn't. There were very few pennies left in my jar at that time.

Disagreements as Opportunities

Conflicts are a normal part of friendships and something we learn how to navigate in early childhood. Disagreements can be opportunities for children to recognize their feelings, accurately communicate them, and express what they need. Some children are naturally skilled at managing, moving past, and avoiding disagreements, while others seem to be magnets for frequent and intense friendship issues.

As we examine how to support children when they have conflicts with friends, we have an opportunity to engage in a parallel process of reflecting on our own professional friendships. Young children argue over possessions, poor communication, taking turns, and a lack of awareness or empathy for each other. Their moods and personal needs—such as hunger, tiredness, or other issues of comfort or feeling secure—also play a role in their disagreements and limit their ability to resolve differences amicably. Helping children verbalize feelings by describing their facial expressions (mirroring) and naming those big feelings are supportive ways to help them during conflicts with friends. We can encourage children to approach their friends and use "I feel" statements, which will be received as less accusatory than "you did" statements. Support children through peer-to-peer relationship issues using the fundamental steps of problem solving, known by therapists as ABCD (Vanbuskirk 2021):

A: Ask, "What is the problem?"
B: Brainstorm solutions.
C: Choose a solution to try.
D: Do it!

Would this strategy have worked for me when I encountered issues with my former friend? It's easier to analyze and evaluate situations when looking back on them than it is when we are in the present moment. Looking back, I don't know if our friendship could have endured the big feelings that I was experiencing. I was angry, hurt, frustrated, sad, and lonely. I wish I had known the SOAR (stop, observe, assess, respond) strategy (Vanbuskirk 2021). The process involves the following steps.

STOP to cool off. Take time for emotion regulation by utilizing a calming strategy, such as deep breathing.

OBSERVE to hear and understand your friend's perspective. Then rate the intensity of the problem.

ASSESS to think about accountability. Take responsibility, if appropriate.

RESPOND by brainstorming possible solutions and compromises. Then choose a solution to try. Affirm the friendship by forgiving, apologizing, or thanking your friend for working with you to find a solution.

How would you use these simple child-friendly strategies as tools for resolving conflicts with professional friends? The first principle of SOAR is to slow down. Rather than rushing to respond immediately to the conflict while you are not emotionally regulated, take time to work on your well-being. In the following scenario, think about the healthiest resolution to the conflict described.

In Your Mind's Eye

Imagine that you work at a child care center near a beautiful conservation area. Every fall the program offers the families a free event called Art in the Park. This year you and your professional friend and another colleague make up the planning committee. The three of you had a meeting, and you suggested a new idea, a transient art experience using natural materials. The committee agrees, and, in addition, the team will set up two more invitations that have been done in the past: tree rubbings and clay creatures. Each of you agrees to manage one of the stations. You collect baskets and begin curating a collection of nature materials. You find out a day before the event that your friends have been working together to plan their invitations, texting back and forth, meeting without you, and leaving you out of decisions. You decide to pour your heart into your invitation and enjoy the day with the children and the families. As you pack up and leave the venue, you don't see your friends. On the way home, you try to process what happened and think about how you will respond.

Invitations in the Forest

Photo Credit: Diane Kashin

Consider the two very different responses featured in table 4.1. They represent extremes and are presented to prompt reflection. How would you respond? Is there a middle ground?

Taking the Time to SOAR	Responding in the Moment
You have proceeded with the event and behaved professionally, focusing on the children and their families. After the event is over, **stop** to take time before agreeing to another collaboration with your friends.	During the event, make sure that your friends are aware that you are mad. If they talk to you, be curt in your reply or walk away. After the event, send them both an email and tell them exactly why you are angry.
Take time to consider what you will say and text, choosing your words carefully to avoid escalation. Work on keeping calm, steady, and stress-free. **Observe** and listen to your friends without shifting to your feelings.	Avoid your friends and find new friends. Make sure your friends know they have hurt you by not talking to them, not responding to texts, and walking out of the room if they walk in. Tell your new friends all about your feelings toward your old friends.
Assess the climate of your professional relationships with these friends over time. Look inward at your feelings and emotions. Decide if you want to go forward without confrontation. If you are emotionally regulated, you may not need to address the issue. If you are going to respond, be kind. Seek closure in a way that focuses on the well-being of all involved.	Start looking for a new job or a transfer to a different site. The climate of your professional relationship is fraught with emotion. Your friends have moved on and have accepted the end of the relationship. Tell your manager what happened so they understand why you need the transfer.
Respond by doing something that you love doing together with your friend, like a walk in the forest. When the time is right, you will know it, and you can approach the issue. Tell your friend that you want to brainstorm ideas to arrive at a consensus about a solution to your differences.	Move on. Ghost your former friends. Put the past behind you. Don't think about it anymore because you have new friends. Spend your free time looking at your former friends' social media posts. When you close your eyes to sleep, replay the event and everything that led to it over and over again.

Table 4.1 Two Possible Responses

When you take time before reacting, you can think, reflect, forgive, and let go. If we avoid responding in the heat of the moment and instead slow down and try to see more clearly, our friendships have a better chance of enduring.

Time for New Friendships

Before our friendship ended, my former friend and I, along with Rosalba, worked together to bring the exhibit *Cultivate the Scientist in Every Child: The Philosophy of Frances and David Hawkins* to Canada. Frances Hawkins was an inspirational early childhood educator. Frances and David knew that if teachers wanted to offer the most optimal learning experiences, they needed to be learners themselves. Teachers, like children, need to mess about. In the words of David Hawkins:

> There is a time, much greater in amount than commonly allowed, which should be devoted to free and unguided exploratory work (call it play if you wish, I call it work). Children are given materials and equipment—things—and are allowed to construct, test, probe, and experiment without superimposed questions or instructions. (Hawkins 2002, 68)

It was a shared interest in Frances and David that led me to meet a new and important friend, Suzanne. Even though many miles separate us, we have now shared many experiences. Our time together has always been playful, but as we engaged in these experiences, our interactions activated our minds. Our experiences together helped me through the grieving process after losing my professional friend.

Featured Friend: Suzanne

I first became aware of Suzanne from her blog, *Interaction Imagination*. We found each other on Facebook, and we bonded over many shared interests, including the work of Frances and David Hawkins. Suzanne traveled from Sweden to meet me, and we shared some experiences that sparked our thinking and dialogue about curriculum and pedagogy. A year later, I went to Sweden, even though I was fearful of traveling alone and still grief-stricken about my former friend. By myself, I took two flights and a bus to reach Suzanne in Stockholm. In a bus full of people conversing in another language, I was worried that I would get off at the wrong stop. When I looked out the window and saw Suzanne, I was so grateful for her open arms. I felt safe. Suzanne had the whole week planned, and every minute was memorable. I am forever grateful that Suzanne has returned to Canada and our shared experiences have led to more deep thinking and pedagogical somersaults. Since I met Suzanne, she has become an accomplished author and speaker. I am not surprised because I could listen to her all day—in fact, I have! I don't feel competitive with Suzanne. I want what is best for her because she is my friend and I love her. I am proud that she is now the author of *The Original Learning Approach* (Axelsson 2022) and that I can call her a true friend.

Selfie with Friends—Laurel, Cindy, Diane, and Suzanne at Lake St. George, Richmond Hill, Ontario (February 2020)

Photo Credit: Diane Kashin

Somersaulting with Friends

In Stockholm Suzanne showed me a book when we were chatting over coffee. Written by Karin Wallin (2003), the title translated into English as *Pedagogical Somersaults: A Book about Swedish Children and the Inspiration from Reggio Emilia*. The message from the title is that children are competent and have more curiosity, talent, strength, imagination, sense, and intelligence than adults imagine. It is adults' locked methods and lack of imagination and curiosity that block the potential of the child. Making an educational somersault in our thoughts means to see from a different perspective than we have before. In the process of reflecting on diverse views and perspectives, our brain does somersaults.

Brain somersaults! What an interesting metaphor that makes me think. Thought-provoking metaphors provide fuel for pedagogical reflections. Like Malaguzzi's *eye jumping over the wall*, metaphors can capture the essence of teaching in a creative, expressive manner that challenges us to see our professional friendships with fresh eyes. "Seeing with fresh eyes" is an idiom that means seeing familiar things as if you've never seen them before. *Fresh eyes*, *jumping eyes*, and *pedagogical somersaults* are examples of figurative language that you can apply to your practice to support reflection.

When I wrote my doctoral dissertation on moving from a theme approach to an emergent curriculum, I chose the metaphor of being on top of a mountain. I saw emergent curriculum as a pathway for early childhood teachers to ascend from a position of poor self-image and sometimes dubious practices to a peak of positive transformation. At the top of the mountain, the early childhood educator finds a reframed self-image. Metaphors can support big thinking about the big ideas of professional friendships. What metaphor can you apply to your professional friendships? Take a few moments to think about it and then draw your metaphor to visually represent your thinking. This is an invitation we can offer children too!

For me, the circle is resonant. The circle as a shape, as a practice, and as a symbol of nature provides early childhood educators with a source of reflection and a catalyst for change. The circle is a common symbol used in many cultures to suggest wholeness, inclusion, femaleness (womb), and eternity. For many Indigenous communities, the circle has a spiritual connotation as the symbol of the moon and the sun. When I think about circles, I make pedagogical connections to the common practice of circle time, which has long been a professional interest of mine. Known by many names, including *group time* and *meeting time*, circle time typically refers to teacher-initiated group experiences. However, when we see the circle as a symbol of divine energy, using *circle time* as a name for experiences that are mandatory, teacher-directed, and developmentally inappropriate creates a disconnect.

Making Connections to Pedagogical Practice: Circles

I wrote my master's thesis on circles (Kashin 1996). To understand circles in practice, I facilitated seven face-to-face sessions with a small focus group of early childhood educators who shared reflections on circle experiences they observed, planned, and implemented. They interviewed colleagues, filled out questionnaires, and journaled. They spoke animatedly of circles that felt painful to endure. As one participant put it, "If a child walks off, you have to realize—yeah, I would have walked off too." At the same time, they shared memories of circles that were joyful, involving laughter, physical movement, music, and full-group participation. They recalled circles that were planned around interactive stories, action songs, games, props, and puppets. These circles lasted a short time and were held in a space large enough for the group size. The children had flexibility; they didn't always sit in a circle formation, and joining the circle was voluntary. In contrast, mandatory circles where children were required to sit in particular ways were described by the participants as difficult and less than joyful.

Provoking Proposal: What are your experiences with circles? How do you avoid mandating circles that make children sit still and listen when they are not wired to do so? What happens when they squirm, play with their shoes, talk out of turn, or engage in other behaviors adults might deem inappropriate?

From my perspective, circles in early learning can be considered metaphorically as broken or open. When children are forced to sit and listen, it does not reflect inclusiveness or equity. This type of circle is broken. However, when we share circles with children that are joyous, they are powerful and impactful. They are spiritually open.

Thinking in a Circle

On one of my first days in Sweden, I witnessed a circle that felt open and powerful as Suzanne facilitated a philosophical dialogue with a group of preschool children. Reflecting on the experience and then discussing it with Suzanne had my brain jumping, leaping, rolling, and percolating. The children were seated on chairs in a circle formation. In the middle on the floor was a bottle of bubbles. They were considering the question, "If you were a forest animal, what kind of animal would you be?" Before the children began the discussion, they decided that they would answer in order rather than randomly.

Three children chose to be a lynx, one picked a wolf, three would be butterflies, and one liked the idea of a bear. One child stated that he had chosen the animal because it could walk on ice, and another child countered to say that other animals could walk on ice. The intent of these philosophical dialogues is for children to be able to discuss, challenge, question, argue, and ultimately listen to the perspectives of others. The thinking about forest animals would continue in the days and weeks to come, and eventually individual choices would shift to one collective choice as the children agreed on one animal for further study and inquiry. At the successful completion of the philosophical dialogue, the children played a bubble game to release the energy resulting from this deep thinking and work of listening (Axelsson 2014a).

When the bubble game was over, I stayed with the children for the rest of the day and for the two days that followed. I saw children who were respected as citizens within a community of learners that included educators and families. I saw adults who viewed the children as competent, capable, and rich in potential, so much so that they believed even young children could engage in philosophical thinking and conflict resolution!

On my first day with the children, I was struck by the beauty of a mural on the wall, and I mistakenly assumed it was a finished product. But on the following day, four children made their way over to the mural and began to paint over their previous work. When the black paint of one child affected the white paint of another, the result was a dialogue about space, color, listening, and rights. This, I learned, was considered a successful outcome of the "together painting" (Axelsson 2014b). I was taken by the realization that the experience was actually an invitation to provoke conversation and an opportunity to address conflict. I thought Suzanne was incredibly brave to intentionally plan to provoke conflict!

From Suzanne's first visit in 2013 to my time in Sweden in 2015 and through Suzanne's return in 2017 and 2020, our time together has exercised our brains with somersaults, playing, and being silly. Suzanne is a wonderful play partner. She is less inhibited than I am, and she inspires me to let go

Painting Together

Photo Credit: Diane Kashin

A Tour of Stockholm Playgrounds with Suzanne

Photo Credit: Diane Kashin

Being Playful

Photo Credit: Diane Kashin

and have fun. She knows that being playful is important for early childhood educators. The research relating to children's play is clear: a playful environment supports development across the physical, emotional, social, language, cognitive, and spiritual domains. Yet the research on the relationship between teachers' and children's playfulness is lacking (Pinchover 2017).

The Healing Value of Play

Play encircles us with comfort when we come together as play partners. Play among professional friends sparks the mind and ignites wonder. Play can also be like a balm to what hurts. Play connects to the self and reveals a place for seeking comfort. Gray (2022) describes soul-enriching play as having these characteristics:

- Play is self-directed, and players are always free to quit.
- Play is activity in which means are more valued than ends.
- Play is guided by mental rules.
- Play is nonliteral, imaginative, and marked off in some way from reality.
- Play involves an active, alert, but non-stressed frame of mind.

Play is therapeutic, and play as a form of therapy is widely used with children. Observing play gives therapists insight into a child's emotions and unresolved trauma. Through play, children learn coping strategies. Play allows professional friends to come together and, for the time, to be active and non-stressed, marked off from reality, and ready to share experiences and build relationships. Research suggests that playing together as professional friends can lead to better teacher-child interactions, which enhance children's playfulness (Pinchover 2017).

Playfulness is our disposition to engage in play. This personality trait exists within and is expressed across all seasons of our lives. Are you a playful early childhood educator? If you aren't, it is never too late to become more playful. Playfulness is usually considered a personal trait, but playful behaviors are skills that can be acquired and honed by playing with our professional friends. Being in a state of play with my friends fills my cup.

Filling Your Empty Cup

When I traveled to Sweden, my emotional cup was almost empty. I am thankful to Suzanne for filling my cup because, as the saying goes, "You can't pour from an empty cup." There is comfort in a full cup of steaming tea or coffee. When we take time to care for ourselves, we can take care of others more effectively. Educators are known to repeatedly empty their cups for the benefit of others while neglecting self-care.

The monk Bernard of Clairvaux (1090–1153) likened self-care to love. We need to love who we are in order to take care of others. Clairvaux speaks of levels of love. The lowest level is selfish love, which targets ourselves above others, and the highest level is caring for ourselves in order to be of benefit to others, a form of self-love (Kohler-Evans 2022). Self-care is not self-seeking with only your own self-interest in mind. We need to take time to replenish. When we feel that we are running on empty, it is time to fill our cup. Joseph and Ravesi-Weinstein (2020) suggest five self-care strategies for teachers, and these have been adapted in figure 4.1.

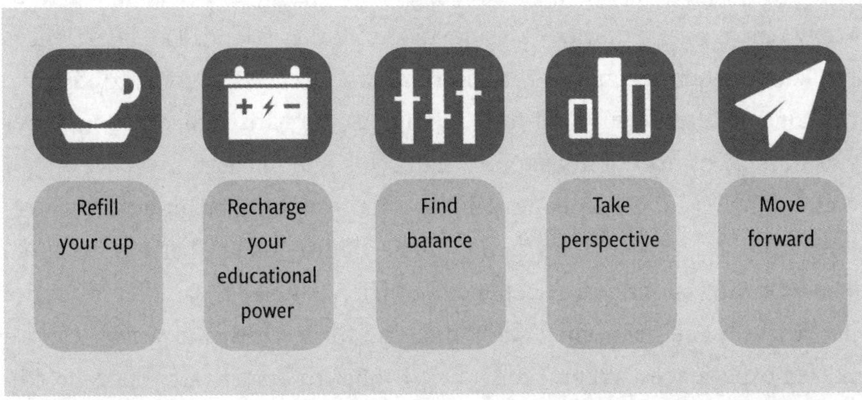

Figure 4.1 Self-Care Strategies

In response to COVID-19, the Housman Institute (2020) suggested that teachers look for ways to address self-care.

- Physical self-care: sleep, eat well, exercise.
- Intellectual self-care: feed your mind.
- Social self-care: have a supportive social network and help others.
- Occupational self-care: seek a work-life balance.
- Emotional self-care: recognize, identify, understand, regulate, and express your feelings and emotions.

Emotional self-care interacts with all the other forms of self-care. With a focus on all areas of self-care, you will have the power to choose how to respond to situations in healthy and productive ways. Self-care is vital to establishing and maintaining professional friendships. Your friends can help you fill your self-care cup. Within a dynamic duo, there will be times when you or your friend need support. Have the metaphorical teapot ready and engage in shared experiences based on shared interests. What might you say to a friend to fill their cup? Consider these suggestions:

- "I am proud to be your friend."
- "I am grateful for our friendship."
- "I enjoy our time together."
- "You are an important part of my life."
- "I appreciate your support."
- "I love sharing ideas with you."
- "The way you think really inspires me."
- "I adore playing with you."

One of my cherished professional friends, Juliet Robertson, is a well-known blogger and outdoor play advocate from Scotland. The experiences we shared when we met at the International Play Association conference in Calgary were playful and fun. Taking a selfie with someone I just met was outside of my comfort zone. I can see some uneasiness in my eyes. I couldn't believe that someone of Juliet's stature would be interested in me. Looking back, I know this was the birth of a friendship that has endured. The following summer we deepened our friendship so that Juliet felt more like a family member when she joined me for a whirlwind week of more shared experiences. When I introduced Juliet to butter tarts during a trip

Selfie with Juliet

Photo Credit: Diane Kashin

to a winery in Niagara Region, the laughs were plentiful and the experience joyful. I will always think of my Scottish friend whenever I take a bite of the syrupy and buttery goodness of the famous Canadian dessert. I am grateful for Juliet beyond measure. She accepted me as a professional friend. These memories are a blessing. She gave me a precious gift.

With Juliet, a butter tart is representative of our friendship. Wildflowers remind me of Laurel, whom you can see in the photo on page 92 with Cindy, Suzanne, and myself. With Laurel, I have shared many experiences in forests and on trails. When Laurel notices a native wildflower growing on the side of the trail, she stops to share knowledge enthusiastically and playfully. It is an infectious experience. When I am with Laurel, I feel her warmth in the same way I do when holding a steaming cup of brew. We are metaphorically sharing a "cuppa," as Laurel would say, every time we are together in the woods.

Playing to Empower

When a person is vulnerable and feels inadequate, they relinquish their power and open themselves up to conflict and stress. Rather than giving away power, play with power to activate your capacity to empower others. Everyone can challenge power imbalances that disempower others. Play along by pretending to hold up a cup of tea. The flowery herbal concoction in your cup of choice is a symbol of friendships. When you sit together and take the time for tea, the banter goes back and forth as each friend gets to feel a sense of control over the dialogue. As your friend speaks, you have an opportunity to consider the virtues they bring to the relationship. Friendships are strengthened and virtues modeled over the cuppas that give us comfort, warmth, and love.

Imagine your friend sitting across from you with a cup in hand. Look into the eyes of your friend. What is commendable about them that makes you want to cultivate the friendship? Consider their virtues as a friend. A *virtue* is a commendable personality trait. Drawing on Aristotle's concept of character friendship, Diana Hoyos-Valdés (2017) suggests in "The Notion of Character Friendship and the Cultivation of Virtue" that good and close relationships help us co-develop commendable personality traits. What virtue does your friend exhibit that you can model? What virtues can you model for your friend? In this way, you are building virtue in your professional friendship. When we are with our professional friends, we are co-developing virtue. We can do this during professional play experiences, or it can happen over a warm beverage as we converse about big ideas.

Big Ideas of Professional Friendships: Play

Play is a big idea of professional friendships. Play should be part of professional learning and the learning of children. Play happens across a spectrum. It is structured by the environment and the materials available indoors and outdoors. The people around us structure play too. According to the *Learning through Play* white paper, "Learning through play can happen through free play *and* when adults or aspects of the environment structure the play situation towards a particular learning goal" (Zosh et al. 2017, 13). Guided play has preplanned learning goals in mind. It is different from free play.

Perhaps the following reflective questions will spark big thinking that invites dialogue with your professional friends.

1. How did you like to play as a child?
2. What were your favorite things to play with as a child?
3. How do you like to play as an adult?
4. What role does play take in your professional learning?
5. What materials do you believe are essential to having optimal play and learning experiences for both children and adults?

6 What is your role during children's play?

7 How do you strike a balance between hands-on and hands-off engagement?

8 How do you advocate for children's play to others?

I don't present the two types of play in opposition, as free versus guided, because I don't want to suggest that one is better than the other or that you have to choose. To engage with this big idea, use continuum thinking to reflect on the spectrum of play. Rather than highlighting differences and engaging in "either/or" thinking, we can avoid judgment by seeking a position along the continuum and discussing our perspectives from a common ground. A continuum highlights our commonalities and is better at depicting a complex topic like play than thinking dichotomously, which would divide the topic into only two parts.

Playing Tea Party

What can you learn about play by playing together with your professional friend? When I played with Suzanne, I realized that I was cautious and inhibited in my play, while she seemed more open to taking risks. Her attitude toward play as an adult appeared to extend to her practice, as she offered children a balanced approach between unstructured free play and guided play. She did not stand back from the play but engaged at times to scaffold children's learning and experiences. Finding a balance between honoring children's autonomous play and scaffolding that play so that it is inclusive and respectful and values all the participants is essential.

Most of my days with Suzanne began with coffee, not tea. However, we both recognize the magic of tea. For years, Suzanne has been the genius behind the International Fairy Tea Party. During this annual event, children and teachers from all over the world celebrate with tea and share photos. The photos often show an invitation that has been set up, the children celebrating, or the aftermath of the experience. The event shows children that they are part of a wider world of play.

The tea party encourages children to slow down and notice what could be evidence of fairies in nature, from small holes in trees to interesting mysterious markings left by insects or animals. It is meant to be fun, but there is deeper meaning in coming together with children to see how we connect over a cuppa. At the tea party, we become open to diverse perspectives, encouraging empathy, understanding other cultures, and valuing imagination. Children (and adults) see how other children (and adults) celebrate around the world.

The Tea Party in the Woods (2015) by Akiko Miyakoshi also encourages deep thinking by children and adults alike because it bridges the divide between reality and fantasy. At the heart of this story is the blurring of what is real and what is imagined. This quietly modernist and whimsical fairy tale reminds us that to be human is to sometimes slip and then wish for a way to magically fix our mistakes.

When Kikko ventures into the woods, she has a blend of courage and reticence along with inquisitiveness. In the woods, she encounters a magical tea party with animals from the forest who help her find her way to her grandma's house. In the end, it is not clear whether Kikko imagined the tea party or the animals simply disappeared back into the woods. This is such a reassuring story about venturing into strange territory alone. The message for readers young and old is that even when travels become hard, we can still discover wondrous things and that friends and help are always available, sometimes where we least expect it.

I have used *The Tea Party in the Woods* to provoke conversations about partnerships. I asked participants how they related to Kikko's experience. Some early childhood educators shared that they needed courage like Kikko to enter the forest, which they liken to a big and unfamiliar school. Some were lost in a forest of conflict and power imbalances with other teachers. On the other hand, some told me about partnerships that developed into friendships with time, love, and support. Metaphorically, it is like the ritual of sharing tea with a friend, as the experience helps us feel well. You feel safe when you share a cup of tea with a friend. Where there is tea, there is hope.

Thank You for Being a Friend

Play was one of the interests I shared with my former friend. We had many shared interests, so it was sad when the friendship was over. Even when a professional friendship ends, you can be grateful for the positive aspects or learning experiences that arose out of the relationship. Counselor and professor Suzanne Degges-White (2018) suggests that there are benefits derived even from negative interactions if we take the time to conduct a "gratitude review":

- List the new things you learned and enjoyed as a by-product of this friendship. List the new experiences you found pleasurable.
- List the negative experiences within this friendship that created disappointment, unhappiness, or other negative emotions and responses.
- List the important things you now recognize as essential in a satisfying relationship.

I now feel thankful to my former friend, and I am filled with kind thoughts and happy memories from our time together. Being thankful for all that I have learned from the relationship has helped me heal. I now recognize that authentically saying thank you often is important. Young children can learn to say thank you, but are they describing feelings of gratitude or just going through the socially prescribed motions? According to Amy Morin (2020), a licensed clinical social worker, psychotherapist, and lecturer, when adults have conversations with children about what it means to be thankful, it can take their understanding of gratitude to a new level. Andrea Hussong (2017), director of the Center for Developmental Science and professor of psychology, suggests that gratitude with children has four parts:

1. What we **NOTICE** in our lives for which we can be grateful.
2. How we **THINK** about why we have been given those things.
3. How we **FEEL** about the things we have been given.
4. What we **DO** to express appreciation in turn.

For children, gratitude should encompass being thankful not just for things but also for relationships. I am grateful to Suzanne for inviting me to learn alongside her and for provoking my thinking to a deeper level. It is through my friends that I have developed into myself. When I play with my friends, I am able to see multiple perspectives that reveal themselves in layers. When we play with materials and ideas, the experiences provoke deeper thinking and reflection.

Four Questions for My Friend: Suzanne

1. **After reading the chapter, what sparked your interest?**

   There is so much to unpack in the chapter, but what strikes me first is the gift of being able to see yourself through someone else's eyes. And isn't that one of the greatest benefits of a professional friend?

I never considered myself brave until you told me so after you watched the "together painting" in action. I never thought of it as brave; I just sensed it was the right thing to do, and yet I think we do need to remind each other of these small, brave steps that allow us to provide children with autonomous play and learning. My autism brings with it a huge amount of anxiety and insecurity, so what I found fascinating is how brave I started to feel and how much easier it became to regulate some of my anxieties once you labeled me *brave*. This gift of being able to see yourself and the world through new eyes is the best part, I think, of a professional friendship. It not only opens up new possibilities but also helps to shut down limiting agendas because you get to see your friends as they are and not as you have been led to believe.

2 **As you considered this spark/interest, how has your thinking moved with it?**

Connecting the sparks of thinking from your chapter with my own Original Learning approach, the term *bravery* relates to many, if not all, of the ten essential threads that are woven into play within that framework. The two that jump out the most are the *risk* and *curiosity* threads, because without being brave, how do we endeavor to include these threads of thinking?

Risk is probably the most obvious one, and there is always risk in friendship, as we don't always know which pathways a friendship will take us or if it will take us places we want to go. A professional friend also brings with it risks, since thinking critically together can bring the risk of change and whatever that change encompasses. It can mean analyzing things that we might not feel comfortable with at first, and we might need to be brave to overcome this discomfort.

Curiosity also requires bravery—to dare to ask questions, seek out new information, try out new things. I have found that allowing others to be curious requires bravery, as maybe they ask questions you don't want them to or their curiosity takes you in directions that you are nervous to pursue. This can happen not only within professional friendships but also as an educator. Allowing curiosity to drive the learning opens up myriad possible pathways that can be taken, and this can feel intimidating at first. I think this is why I prefer projects rooted in wonder, as it allows myriad curiosity paths that we can all explore together, while the wonder creates a sense of belonging and togetherness in the midst of our differences. It is actually in the curiosity chapter of my book that I mention you, Diane—and the value our professional friendship has for me—and ponder the idea that maybe we all need a curious friend too. In my chapter, I liken it to the phenomenon of "lawn-mower parents" and the idea that they cut down all the grass to make things easier for their children, but with a twist. I am not encouraging educators to mow the meadow of play and learning to make it easy, because then we would not need to be brave. Instead, I raise the idea that if the grass is very long, maybe as educators we need to mow some pathways so that children can make new discoveries and then continue to macheté their own way. I also point out that sometimes it feels like educators have made themselves a wonderful area within the tall grass that becomes so comfortable that they never move beyond it. A curious friend, then, is one who cuts down a pathway so that other wonders, knowledge, interactions, and discoveries can be made.

Sometimes we are just too tired or too scared to be curious alone, and having a friend in this can help. I think that a friend could/should be both curious and critical, because isn't this what being a critical friend is rooted in—being curious to know more, being curious to understand the how, why, and when? The etymological root of *curious* is *cura*, meaning "care"; we care enough about something to find out more, we care about our friendship. And I most certainly do, Diane.

3 **After considering questions one and two, what connections are you making to your own experiences with professional friends?**

I consider myself a wealthy person indeed when it comes to professional friends. Not only do I value that I have so many, but I am enriched because they can be found all over the world. I have been invited to walk so many pathways, many of which I would probably never have discovered by myself; and for this, I am extremely grateful. The treasure of multiple perspectives, the gift of being exposed to cultures, stories, and experiences so unlike my own childhood and adulthood, and the reward of unpacking stereotypes and prejudice through listening open up my map of possible destinations to visit and routes to get there a hundredfold.

4 **What advice can you give to the readers of this book to help them on their journeys with professional friends?**

My advice is simple and yet complex: slow down, look closely, and listen deeply. All three take practice. One of the ways I have practiced slowing down is by taking close-up photographs of all sorts of things, mostly things from nature, such as plants, bugs, and animals. Slowing down to be able to notice, and being more consciously aware of this slower feeling, has helped me recognize when I am in too much of a hurry or too stressed to be able to notice or listen properly to others, both as an educator and also as a professional friend. As a professional friend, we need to know how to listen to understand, not just hear the words and wait for a silence to start talking, but to really *look* closely at what is being said because we listen with more than our ears.

I have been using the hashtags #slowdown, #lookclosely, and #listendeeply as a way to show people that this is something that I have done for a long time and continue to practice doing, as it is not something that is just learned but must be maintained. Maybe it is a kind of mindfulness, to be open to what is happening right now without an agenda besides noticing what the world has to offer. I never thought of it as mindfulness until I described what I was doing in the forest to my mother-in-law, that is, listening to the trees as my professional friends. This requires me to let go of all the noisy thoughts in my head so I can listen to the forest, and she commented that it was a kind of mindfulness. It's not easy, since I find thoughts sneaking in every once in a while, and they can be quite loud so I can't hear the forest (not just the sounds but the energy too). I think this is also an important part of professional friendship, being open to truly hearing what is being said and not allowing your agenda to warp the intention of what is being shared to fit your own theories.

I read this chapter three times before I could answer the questions. The first time was fast, but I was so excited because I was seeking out my name and wanted to know what you wrote, so I was not open to noticing everything. I needed to slow down and look closely at all the words and stories. By the third time, I was able to start "listening" to what was being conveyed. I am not suggesting that everyone needs to read books or chapters three times, but simply that the listening part of professional friendship is complex. I can't wait for the book to be completed, to see how things evolve together with your editor, as isn't that yet another critical friendship that helps you refine words and phrases so that others can fully understand and appreciate the story being told? I know I have valued my editor, Melissa, whose suggestions and questions enabled my book to be more *me*. I think society frequently forgets that together we are stronger and that collectively we can be more ourselves.

—Suzanne Axelsson

Chapter Five

Constructing Friendships

MAKING CONNECTIONS

Hello, Friend!

After considering the friends featured in each chapter, has your perspective about professional friendships changed? You may now see professional friendships from a more layered and complex position, yet it is important to recognize that you will never arrive to a place where you can see it all. Our perspectives continue to multiply and diversify as we engage in shared experiences with our friends. Perspective is an attitude or point of view that gets richer, more complex, and deeper the more open we are to multiple viewpoints. Multiple perspectives promote both a sense of group membership and the uniqueness of self. We have a responsibility to try to see from different perspectives.

If we consider constructing friendships to be like constructing a building, we know that friendships need to be built upon a solid foundation. That foundation is you. It all connects back to you. In this chapter, we recognize that while some friendships will last a lifetime and others will come to an end, the person who greets you in the mirror every morning will be there forever. You are the first layer in a layered perspective. We are coming back to the self, but the self in relationship to others. The world we live in is complex, and the relationships we have are nuanced. This chapter is also about perspective taking, finding agency in professional learning, giving and receiving feedback, and slowing down so we can see many layers.

Children's books offer prompts for perspective taking that can be used by people of all ages to reflect on friendships. When we see through the lens of a favorite book, we are provoked by a new perspective. Books help us practice cognitive flexibility as they change the focus of our attention to someone else. We practice inhibitory control when taking the perspective of others. We can collaboratively or individually determine how someone else feels through books, and therefore practice empathy.

Agates provide another metaphor for perspective taking and the layers of relationships. An agate is a semiprecious gemstone with layers or bands of colors. Agates form within other rocks when silica-rich water flows into cavities and solidifies. An agate develops only through interactions with other rocks, much as we develop into ourselves through interactions with others. Like an agate, we have layers of complexity.

Perspective taking, according to early learning expert Ellen Galinsky (2010), involves distinct and significant skills for children. Consider, while reading the bullet points below, how these skills are also important in the cultivation of professional friendships.

- Determining how someone else feels: trying to figure out how another person is feeling or thinking.
- Inhibitory control: putting our own thoughts on hold to engage in perspective taking and think about the world from someone else's point of view.
- Cognitive flexibility: switching up our perspectives by looking outside the box of our normal thinking.

In 2016 I was invited by Lisa Burman (2023) to present a series of workshops in Adelaide, Australia. On the one hand, the invitation felt like the realization of a dream. On the other hand, even thinking about the possibility seemed impossible and scary. Alone, I didn't feel confident enough to take on the challenge before me. Cindy reached out to offer her services as a traveling companion and co-facilitator. My confidence soared, and we shared a joyful experience of a lifetime. We both agree that the greatest gifts from our time in Australia were the friendships formed that now endure. We gratefully welcomed Lisa, Dannielle, Amanda, and Mimi into our circle of professional friends.

In Australia we shared a perspective-taking experience inspired by agates. Not knowing much about the context of our audience, we were impressed that the educators were sitting together as learning teams, each supported by an identified critical friend. The assignment for the critical friend was to facilitate the development and growth of the team during the session and

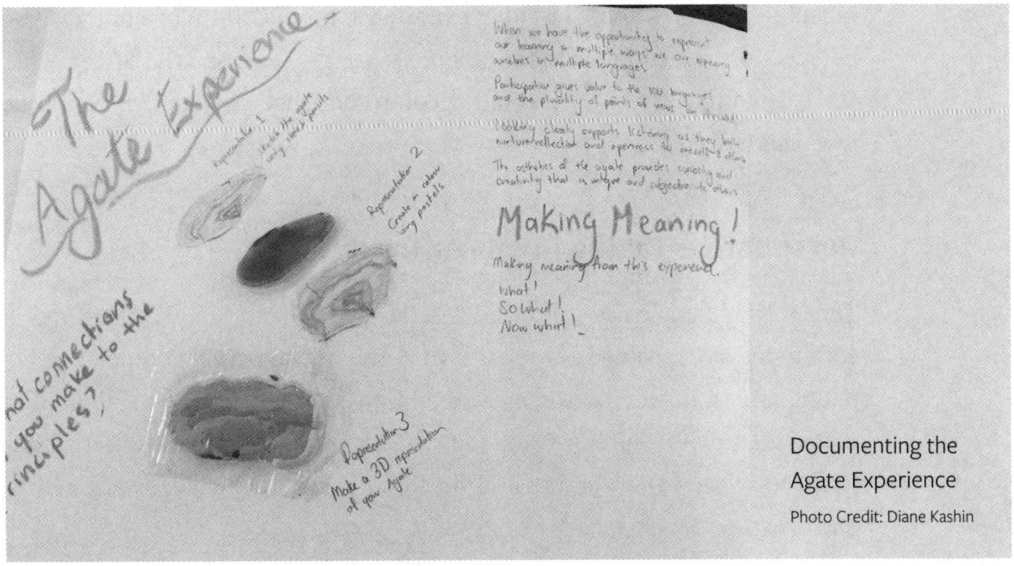

Documenting the Agate Experience

Photo Credit: Diane Kashin

over time. To support reflection, each table had large sketchbooks that the groups used to collaboratively document their professional learning experience. At different points during the day, the team members added their thoughts and reflections.

As I facilitated the agate experience with Cindy, it was illuminating to see how the participants were representing and reflecting their ideas. When we invited the educators to add light and zoom in, the idea was to defamiliarize the object in hand. *Defamiliarizing* is an artistic technique for presenting common things in an unfamiliar or strange way to enhance our perception of the familiar. The strategy works with people of all ages. Looking closely at objects offers children the opportunity to engage in defamiliarization. When we use a camera to zoom in for a close-up, we see details that were otherwise hidden.

As participants represented the agate through sketching and pastels, as well as three dimensionally using a modeling paste, they looked closely and saw fine details, recognizing uniqueness and complexity. Each agate is different, just as every teacher and every child and every context is individual. The agate experience demonstrates complexity and celebrates diversity. The outer edge of an agate is rough and common, but inside there is singular beauty revealed in layers.

In the end, we gifted each participant with the agate that they had depicted in multiple ways. We hoped that it would evoke memories of a joyful and meaningful professional learning experience grounded in love and diverse perspectives, reflecting both the uniqueness of the agate and the agate bearer. We trusted that the agates would become cherished objects that would be loved and cared for.

Perspective Taking Involves Trust

Teresa Draguicevich (2021), who teaches at Innovations Academy and is cofounder of Learning Journeys Forum, investigated trust and perspective taking after a debate between two children erupted and then spilled over to an entire class. She suggested that children learn that trust is fundamental to all relationships and that honoring another's beliefs does not negate one's own.

> The roots of this trust start in infancy, through relationships or attachment with primary caregivers. The foundation expands during early childhood through relationships with key figures, including early childhood educators, who can guide children toward *interpersonal trust.* (64)

Interpersonal trust involves a willingness to accept vulnerability or risk, based on your expectations of another person's behavior. How much can you rely on what your friend says or does? Children need time in relationships to discern trustworthiness. In their relationships, they learn

- who can they count on,
- who consistently and sensitively cares about them, and
- who offers them accurate information about their world.

Like trust, perspective taking develops over time and is influenced by experience. Children need time to identify and discuss their own and others' thoughts, feelings, and actions. They gradually come to understand that differences exist. This helps them to form and keep friendships. Early childhood educators can take an active role in fostering children's perspective-taking skills by

- using intentional language to model inclusivity,
- designing invitations to provoke children to "benefit from and depend on the expertise of others" (Edwards, Gandini, and Forman 1998, 302),

- sharing books that feature diverse perspectives and cultures, and
- building a safe community to express and accept differing perspectives (Draguicevich 2021).

A six-month study to gain a deeper understanding of how to increase trust and perspective taking in the classroom ensued, and these four pedagogical strategies are offered by Draguicevich and depicted in figure 5.1:

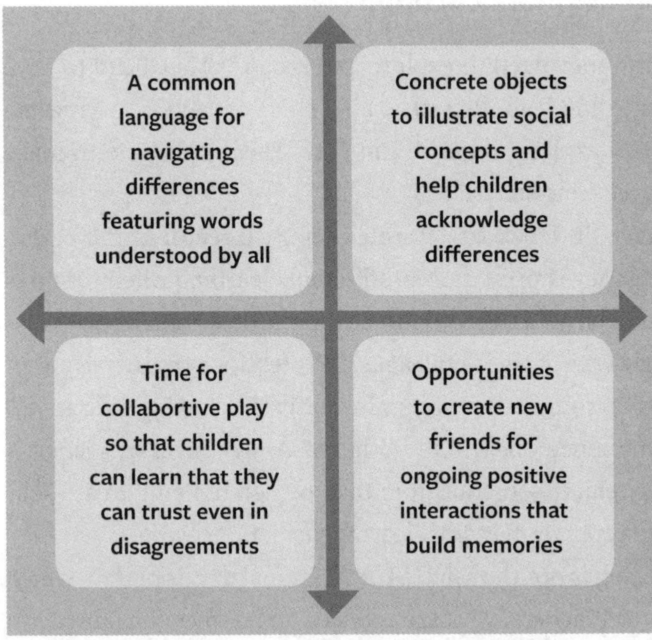

Figure 5.1 Pedagogical Strategies to Build Trust

In a parallel process, early childhood educators can look at trust and perspective taking within their professional friendships. Inspired by this important example of action research, these questions offer you an invitation to consider your practice:

1. Who among your professional friends can you count on to consistently care about you with sensitivity?
2. Can you trust your friend to offer you a different perspective and be open to yours?
3. How do you know if your friend has the same level of trust with you?
4. What shared experience can you have with your friend that will depend on and benefit from the other's expertise?
5. What language can you intentionally use in your relationship to navigate differences?

6. What books and concrete objects can you use to illustrate complex social concepts and respectfully acknowledge differences?
7. When and how can you make time for collaborative play and inquiry with your friend?
8. How can you expand your perspective taking?

Agency in Professional Learning

For children to learn, they need to explore and inquire. They need to have agency to self-initiate and lead their play. Like children, adults learn when they have freedom to explore, inquire, and play. They need time to make connections so the learning sticks.

According to Anne O'Brien (2016), former deputy director of the Learning First Alliance, agency is present in professional learning when teachers act purposefully and constructively to direct their professional growth and contribute to the growth of their colleagues. Professional agency is often referred to as "making choices among alternatives," "taking initiative," or "being able to influence oneself and others." A high level of agency is involved when early childhood educators take ownership and create self-initiated and self-directed professional learning experiences.

Professional learning is not the same as professional development, which is something done to teachers, who are reduced to passive consumers. In a seminal study, Alma Fleet and Catherine Patterson (2001) speak of the importance of educators owning their own ideas rather than just receiving knowledge from someone else. This aligns with a constructivist perspective, which recognizes that learners construct knowledge rather than just passively taking in information. It is by experiencing the world within our early childhood education ecosystems and by reflecting on those experiences that we build our own knowledge. Professional learning is situational and contextual. You are the expert in your own context, and you have a significant perspective that should be heard.

When you abdicate ownership in your professional learning by allowing others to decide for you which workshops or webinars to take, you reduce your ownership in your own growth. When others assign professional learning experiences to you and make decisions for you, do you know what they are thinking when they decide? Are they looking for a particular focus or subject that they have identified as missing from your practice? That approach uses a deficit model that looks to fill gaps. Instead, why not build on strengths or interests?

What are your professional interests? All my professional friends share an interest in play. We move with this interest together by playing with materials and ideas and by connecting to invitations from Mother Earth. This is self-directed, reflective, and collaborative professional inquiry, and we are constructing our own knowledge by taking the time to move and mess about as self-directed learners.

Psychologist and play advocate Peter Gray (2016) contends that children have it in their DNA to be self-directed learners, especially in the absence of adult control. Children continually practice making plans and carrying them out. They make mistakes and learn from them. If children are wired to be self-directed learners, can we rewire ourselves as adult learners? Self-directed learning offers you control and ownership over your learning. It gives you the opportunity to choose learning activities that are relevant and meaningful to your professional practice (College of Early Childhood Educators 2017). Self-directed learning is empowering, especially when it is undertaken with friends! When we engage in professional learning with our friends, it is an opportunity to learn collaboratively. The cyclical view from the Seasonal Pedagogy (Martin 2021) provides a prompt to consider self-directed learning. Follow along, beginning with the spark that ignites your professional wonders.

- *Birth*: Observe and reflect on your practice. What is sparking your professional curiosity? What do you wonder about children's learning and your own? Is there a seed that needs germinating?
- *Movement*: Move with your learning by taking the time and attention needed for the seed to sprout. Engage all your senses while you direct your own path forward. The seed will grow with a connection between theory and practice. Document your engagement and reflect on your experience.
- *Relationships*: Interpret the children's learning and your own. What are the developing relationships or connections?
- *Passing*: How will you share what you learned in the spirit of giving back? Tell the story of your learning. What ignited your interest, how did you build relationships, and—now—how can you pass it on to others? What story can you document and share? In the process, more stories will need to be told, and you begin again at *Birth*.

Be the Power

To be knowledgeable about and interested in professional topics as they relate to your practice is to have power. When using the term *power*, I am not referring to power over others but power to empower others and yourself. With knowledge comes power. Research describes stories of critical friends supporting each other and finding power within themselves in a work environment that often leaves them feeling powerless (Brewer, Wideman-Johnston, and McCabe 2021). Professional friendship offers the means to change our stories.

Miriam Beloglovsky (2022) is a prolific early learning author who has a wide range of professional interests but has written most extensively about the topic of loose parts. *Loose parts* are materials that children can move, manipulate, control, and change while they play. They can carry, combine, redesign, line up, take apart, and put back together loose parts in almost endless ways. Loose parts invite conversations and interactions, encouraging collaboration and cooperation. They possess infinite play possibilities (Daly and Beloglovsky 2015). At the time of this writing, I have yet to meet Miriam in person, but she is my professional friend. The kindness she has extended has been empowering. I recognize from Miriam that I have the power to write my own story going forward. Miriam is the featured friend of this chapter.

My relationship with Miriam has helped me acknowledge that I am powerful, and I can share my power while being kind to myself. Kindness has the power to sustain professional relationships so that they can grow into professional friendships.

The Yin and Yang Perspective

A narrative of a kind friendship must start with ourselves. When you're self-critical, your inner voice will always cut you down, undermining your ability to be happy and your capacity to be a friend. We need self-compassion to stay friendly with others over the long term. Self-compassionate people are not selfish. They are connected to others. They know that everyone struggles and that we all make mistakes. People with self-compassion practice *self-kindness*, the quality that leads us to give ourselves the same care we give to others. You can learn not to attack or abandon yourself if you fall short. Instead, you can learn to offer yourself words of warmth and unconditional acceptance.

Kristin Neff, a professor and researcher, is the author of *The Yin and Yang of Self-Compassion: Cultivating Kindness and Strength in the Face of Difficulty* (2019). The yin side of self-compassion is related to acceptance and reassurance. The yang is about the actions required. From the perspective of professional friendship, think of a colleague who is struggling with work-life balance. She received a warning about taking private phone calls at work. A compassionate friend would never say, "Don't worry, it's nothing. We all get written up every now and then. I still love you." This response negates your colleague's feelings. A compassionate friend will give unconditional love but will also want their friend to achieve a work-life balance because they want their friend to be happy. A compassionate friend will look for ways to help their friend. Now apply the same yin and yang to yourself. What could you say to yourself when you are struggling, as we all do in our lives? What words would be accepting and reassuring? What words could you offer yourself to help you identify actions that you could take?

In Your Mind's Eye

Imagine that you are asked by your employer to facilitate a workshop experience for a group of colleagues. You want to provide a hands-on experience for them that they could do with children. After looking online and thinking about possibilities, you settle on a painted-rock activity. You proceed to collect rocks from a local beach. You suggest to your fellow teachers that, once painted, the rocks can be left around the playground for the children to find. This, you suggest, will spark the children's interest, and the teachers could set up a similar painting experience for them. The workshop goes well, and the rocks are placed in the playground before the children awake from their nap. You feel very proud and accomplished, so you are shocked when you are given feedback by your program's pedagogical leader, questioning your choices. You are told that painting the rocks has obscured their inherent beauty and disconnects children from nature. How would you apply a yin-yang framework to this scenario?

Painted Rocks

Photo Credit: Diane Kashin

Beach Collecting

Photo Credit: Diane Kashin

The story of the painted rocks is based on a personal experience I had with Cindy. Very early on in our friendship, we both worked as coordinators at different campuses of the same college, and we attended the same conference. I missed the first part of the session, which featured rocks with words painted on them. When I arrived, Cindy handed me a rock with the word *integrity* because she thought of me when she saw it. I have received many gifts from friends, but this one is especially meaningful. I still have it all these years later. It signifies a friendship that has endured and prospered.

With Cindy, I had the shared experience of collecting rocks for workshops while beachcombing along a lakeshore. Lovingly lugging these treasures back with us, we would then invite teachers to adorn their rocks with one meaningful power word. What would be your power word? Today I would choose *self-compassion*, to represent the yin. I accept myself as evolving. I can be kind to myself. Years later, Cindy asked Gokoomis Jacque about the practice of writing and painting on rocks. Her answer was simple: "Rocks are already beautiful." From the yang side, I engaged in rethinking the rock experience, and I took action. I stopped painting on rocks and offering the experience during workshops. I can use this experience as an opportunity to improve. Why obscure the beauty that is already in nature? I have the power to change. My yang power word would be *powerful*.

Big Ideas of Professional Friendships: Shared Interests

Developing shared interests is a powerful way to solidify a friendship that can last a lifetime. Loose parts, like rocks, represent an interest that I share with many professional friends. These incredible open-ended materials can inspire play among professional friends, cultivating a shared interest within a common identity.

In the conversations I have had with Cindy about loose parts, we recall the early-career transformational experience of reading landscape architect and researcher Simon Nicholson's seminal article, "How NOT to Cheat Children: The Theory of Loose Parts" (1971). Together we discussed how this article could influence our practice in teaching early childhood education, and we decided to initiate a dialogue with our colleagues about changing our current pedagogical approach. There was opposition from some, which was difficult to receive, but together we prevailed. We also incorporated loose parts in our classes for adult students so they could experience the subject of play and learning concretely. We reiterated to our colleagues and students that the theory of loose parts was a *theory*. We did this to counter the ever-present request for a simple definition of loose parts. We wanted there to be rich and deep dialogue so that the college-level early childhood education students could develop their own theories in the abstract. The theory of loose parts constitutes a professional interest that I share with many friends. The power of shared interests as a big idea of professional friendships cannot be underestimated. Loose parts brought Miriam, a new friend, into my life.

Featured Friend: Miriam

For over twenty years, Miriam has been engaged in a journey to explore play and loose parts. She has researched the application of loose parts in early childhood ecosystems and has authored five books on that topic alone. She consults, designs, coaches, and teaches on the subject of loose parts. She is a giant on whose shoulders I stand. When Miriam asked me to be part of an online Loose Parts Summit, I was both flattered and afraid. I was intimidated and fearful of receiving negative feedback again. My understanding of the theory continues to evolve. I do not consider myself an expert. When two experts commented in the past to make corrections or suggestions, my reaction was defensiveness and hurt. Was I brave enough to do it again? I decided I was, realizing that the passing of time had allowed me to reflect and grow from this feedback. When I met Miriam online, I was nervous, but she was kind and encouraging. I felt immediately comfortable to share my perspectives, and Miriam took the time to listen. She even suggested that I should write a book! It is through Miriam that I have been able to take this journey of exploring friendships in early childhood education. My gratitude is overwhelming, and I am at a loss for words to express myself. Has this ever happened to you?

Professional dialogues about shared interests are gifts I have received from countless friends. They gave their perspectives and their time. They offered an ear and showed genuine interest in my perspectives. It is from each and every one of these conversations that I have developed into myself. At times, I am overwhelmed by the magnitude of meaning that has come from generous professional friends who have shared their perspectives and feedback.

Sharing Feedback

Giving feedback and receiving it from others is an ongoing part of professional friendships. The way we give and receive feedback ourselves is a significant component of being self-compassionate. A healthy friendship needs two healthy individuals to achieve its fullest possibilities. Miriam is the epitome of a professional friend. Our relationship is not competitive but supportive. When I had shared with her that I found negative feedback difficult to receive, she was reassuring and kind. I had posted a blog about loose parts and described an experience I provided to teachers that I called the "loose parts buffet" (Kashin 2018). I explained that my intention was to demonstrate the sustainability of these materials while supporting the idea of creating rather than consuming. I had pipe cleaners, elastics, wool, and modeling paste available because of their ability to connect the various materials. Participants would creatively transform the loose parts in ways that could be dismantled. The materials were then returned to the buffet, to live to play another day.

The Loose Parts Buffet

Photo Credit: Diane Kashin

I had been inspired by early childhood experts Margie Carter and Deb Curtis, who stated that "children really deserve an environment stocked with open-ended materials and loose parts, things from nature as well as the recycle bin. When we offer children these kinds of materials, they become creators of their experiences rather than consumers" (Carter and Curtis 2012, 93). Someone suggested that I reconsider the message this abundance of mostly purchased loose parts was sending. From a sustainability and accessibility perspective, I was conveying the idea that if you had money, you could purchase loose parts rather than reinforcing the truth that large collections of loose parts are not needed and often nature and the recycling bin can provide low-cost options. Even though the feedback was gently offered, I perceived it as criticism.

In the baskets, I had enough materials for hundreds of participants, some of which I had collected and some of which had been donated by suppliers. By not offering glue that would turn these materials into products, I thought I was sending a message that we could experience the loose parts in a way that they would not be consumed. Yet here I had shared this photo on social media, and the message was not clearly conveyed, and others saw the image in a different way. It gave me pause, and I reflected and recognized that there was another layer, another perspective, that I could be open to. I can consider the feedback of others without it hurting my feelings. I can separate my professional learning from my ego.

Ask yourself and then ask your friend these questions to cultivate your professional friendship:

1. If you receive critical feedback, how can a yin-yang perspective support your sense of self?
2. How can you give the gift of time to yourself?
3. How can you use the yin-yang perspective to support your friend's sense of self?
4. How can you give the gift of time to your friend?
5. If you were to gift yourself a power word, what would it be?
6. If you were to gift your friend a power word, what would it be?
7. Do you have a particular professional interest?
8. How can you seek multiple perspectives to broaden and deepen your understanding of your interest?

I feel grateful when my friends share their perspectives and listen to mine in a friendly way. Being friendly is a component of professional friendships. If someone is friendly, they behave in a pleasant, kind way and like to be with others. Being friendly has not always been easy for me, and upon reflection, I see that my past inability to act in this way related to a lack of self-compassion and the ever-present imposter syndrome. I avoided eye contact and lacked the confidence to smile. I held back. Reflecting on past relationships has helped me to recognize ways that I can improve and give back. Going forward, I can and will be more friendly. I can give more gifts of smiles. I can also thank others for friendship and learning.

Gifts are not always easily given or received. I find gift giving to be stressful when associated with birthdays and holidays. I don't celebrate Christmas. It is not part of my family heritage. I have not had the experience of seasonal gift buying for friends, family, and those who provide services. It isn't something that I miss. I do, however, love receiving unexpected gifts from friends at random times. When a friend tells me, "This made me think of you," it makes me happy. When I find a gift for a friend that makes me think of them, it too is a heartfelt experience. Out-of-the-blue gift giving can strengthen friendships. I have cherished mementos that I unexpectedly received from friends. I also love when my friends slow down and give me the gift of their time.

Slowing Down

What are the benefits of slowing down? Early years researchers Kari Carlsen and Alison Clark (2022) have studied children and teachers engaged in slow pedagogies, intertwined as learners. They cite David Elkind (2001), who expressed concerns about "the hurried child" in the 1980s. A slow pedagogy happens when learners are in "full engagement in the flow of deep time" (Carlsen and Clark 2022, 203), and this connects to psychologist Mihaly Csikszentmihalyi's (1997) concept of *flow*, a state in which there is such deep engagement in an experience that nothing else seems to matter. It is so joyful that we would do it for the sheer sake of doing it.

Carlsen and Clark (2022, 209) describe this slow pedagogy as "catching the moment," where teachers give their full attention to the present, suspending other agendas, concerns, and plans for the time being. This is done while "stretching time," which gives children and teachers a chance to breathe. What if we looked at professional friendship through the lens of slow pedagogies?

As a pedagogical approach, emergent, inquiry-based learning is about slowing down and allowing a natural process to emerge. Planning and programming in a cyclical and seasonal way allows for a holistic approach to children's play and learning. The Seasonal Pedagogy offers inspiration for beginning the process.

- *Birth* is observation. Begin with observation, which can be the birth of an inquiry that grows from children's authentic interests.
- *Movement* is documentation. Offer extended time for the children to move with their interests as you document them, balancing being present with capturing images and recording the play.
- *Relationships* is interpretation. Interpret the documentation based on the connections or relationships that you, the children, and the land are revealing. Ask for interpretations from others to create more threads in the web of connections.
- *Passing* is programming. Plan the pedagogical path ahead and pass on the story of the play and learning to others.

From the perspective of professional collaboration and co-inquiry, consider this example. Your teaching partner introduces a book to the children while you observe what you see and what you hear. You share your notes analytically while trying to discern children's authentic interests that are worthy of pursuing. Once identified, you engage the children to hear their perspectives and learn about their prior experience and knowledge. You may need to modify or change your ideas because you are open to these many perspectives.

Guided play invitations and free-play experiences based on children's interests offer opportunities to document how children move with their ideas over time. When we interpret notes, photos, and videos with others, we are realizing connections and relationships, as demonstrated in the four-season cattail experience I shared in chapter 3. As we continue to accumulate, share, and add to the documentation over time, the relationships between people and with the land are formed and reformed and reveal themselves. You will know organically in an emergent way how to continue the cyclical process. This is a natural way to program, in the rhythm of Mother Earth's seasons of life.

Thank You for Being a Friend

I have looked up to those whom I consider giants in early childhood education. I recognize their influence in shaping who I have become. I am grateful to all the giants who have helped me see further. I am particularly thankful to Margie Carter and Deb Curtis. In 2005 I realized that the professional learning I wanted and needed was not available in my area. I reached out to Margie, and with Rosalba and two other inspiring friends, Heather and Evette, we organized not one but two conferences as the Acorn Collaborative, featuring the dynamic duo of Deb and Margie.

Margie and Deb are professional friends for all early childhood educators. I am thankful to Margie and Deb for working with our little collaborative so we could have these unforgettable shared experiences. I am grateful to my fellow "nuts" at the Acorn Collaborative for sharing the risk of planning conferences, something we had only a little bit of experience with. Margie wrote about rethinking conference learning in an article and offered special appreciation to a number of people and their colleagues who took up the challenge and hosted. I was and am honored to be included on the list (Carter 2006).

Thinking Back

In 2004 I attended the National Association for the Education of Young Children (NAEYC) conference when it was held in Toronto. I remember heading south and driving into the busyness of the downtown core to the conference center, which was overwhelming in size. I was nervous parking and worried that I wouldn't locate the conference or my parked car at the end of the day. I was sorry that I didn't have a friend with me. I managed to find my way, and the trade show was the first place I headed. I was on a mission to buy more books written by Margie and Deb. *Training Teachers: A Harvest of Theory and Practice* (2002) had been transformational to my practice as a relatively new early childhood education professor. With my hands full of books, I was standing in line to pay for my purchases when I noticed a colleague who also had an armful of Margie and Deb books. As we stood there, comparing our piles and offering each other our enthusiastic reviews of the titles we had read, others (strangers) joined in the conversation. It was an unforgettable experience and the beginning of one of my most significant professional friendships. Yes, it was my former friend, and this was the birth of our relationship.

My former friend was there for me during the season of my life when it all began. As I moved through the years, expanding my perspectives on early childhood education, there were many memorable moments. I wonder if she remembers hearing Margie Carter read *Roxaboxen*, a beautiful story by Alice McLerran (1991) and illustrated by Barbara Cooney, about loose parts, play, and the seasons of our lives.

Based on a true event about a group of friends and the imaginary town they create using found materials, the book is about the power of imagination, the transformational possibilities of loose parts, and the changing seasons of our lives. It is a timeless story of play, agency, creativity, collaboration, friendship, and aging. In the end, the tale refers to the changing of the seasons and reminds us that when we are children, we notice the seasons, but the years seem to last forever. As we get older, the years fly by, and if we don't pay attention to the seasons, we won't notice them changing. In 2000 the actual site of *Roxaboxen* was turned into a park that was kept close to the original so children could continue to use their imaginations.

Take time to slow down and consider the story of *Roxaboxen*. This book can propel a parallel process of critical reflection and offer you and children sparks for inquiry. Consider time, materials, people, and places as you think about the following:

1. How might this book encourage conversation between professional friends?
2. How might it inspire children to be creators rather than consumers?
3. What is needed for children to create their own *Roxaboxen* in their own contexts?

For me, as someone who is in the winter season of their life, this is a reminder to slow down, look closely, and notice the gifts of the seasons that we receive daily from Mother Earth, our friends, and our families. The children of *Roxaboxen* did not need adult direction to create memories that lasted a lifetime and that could be passed down from generation to generation. All they needed were loose parts.

Loose parts have the capacity to bring intergenerational joy. I believe they are my fountain of youth! *Roxaboxen* has inspired me to play with loose parts and to pass on my love of loose parts to my grandchildren. Wesley will soon join his brother, Griffen, and cousin, Reese, in discovering the possibilities for play that Bubbie's house affords! It is my sincere hope that all my grandchildren will carry these memories with them throughout their lives.

Four Questions for My Friend: Miriam

1 **After reading the chapter, what sparked your interest?**

I first have to say that I was moved by this chapter's connection to compassion and listening to diverse perspectives. It takes time to develop the willingness to listen to what other people have to share, specifically when you have to let go of your own ideas and understandings. The concept of self-compassion is crucial to our work. I tend to be hard on myself, constantly searching for the "best." Being reminded to have self-compassion, give myself permission to make mistakes, and slow down helps me focus on what is essential and think about how to be a better professional friend. We also have the responsibility to be grounded in our own selves. I guess the idea of professional friendships is based on the ongoing co-construction of separate and collaborative perspectives.

Essential friendship is not designed to change the other person. Instead, it is an exchange and a responsibility to build each other up and to trust that each person will give freely when they are ready. This is a risk because it requires us to walk that tightrope between our experiences and the fear of being hurt. I think this is when self-compassion is essential. Self-compassion allows us to learn to trust and offer grace to the other person. When I first reached out to Diane to present at the Loose Parts Summit, I felt intimidated. I admired her work from afar, and I would constantly think to myself, "How come I could not come up with that brilliant thought?" I think many friendships begin with mutual respect for each other's work. I continue to be in awe of Diane's writing, so for me, it was comfortable to slip into a relationship of trust.

2 **As you considered this spark/interest, how has your thinking moved with it?**

Part of self-compassion is to set boundaries that help us maneuver difficult situations. Painfully, sometimes we learn to let go of people whom we consider to be our professional friends. Boundaries remind us to continue to be self-compassionate and to stay grounded in our integrity and willingness to give to others with kindness and grace. My thinking is always evolving and constantly changing. When I read this chapter, I made some connections to how some of my professional friend relationships ended. I wonder what I could have done differently. Now I know that self-compassion could have helped me set boundaries and create a more authentic way of interacting with others. Lately, I have been thinking about my friendships and what sustains them. I believe that trusting who I am and authentically showing up for my friends has helped me nurture and cultivate meaningful friendships in my life. I can be friends with many people, but I can only be a critical friend to those who are willing to trust and show up in their authentic way while letting my authentic self freely emerge.

3 **After considering questions one and two, what connections are you making to your own experiences with professional friends?**

There are times when I keep professional relationships at arm's length. For me, it is a matter of trusting people and being able to know that they will uphold and protect the confidentiality of the friendship. Unfortunately, I have trusted professional friends only to discover that they have taken my intellectual property and used it for their own benefit. That has deeply affected the way I see professional friendships. However, I also have learned that I must stay true to my own integrity and let go of friendships that do not support my identity. I come to this point with empathy, compassion for myself, and an understanding that there will always be people in the world who need to take from others rather than generate their own content and materials. My experience with professional friends has taught me to trust myself and not rely on other people's constant support. I have become more discerning about who I consider a professional friend, thinking critically about how we can support each other. A professional friendship requires duality and an honest give-and-take. When the relationship is too one-sided, an issue of power emerges, creating distrust and eventually eroding the friendship. When I enter a relationship with honesty, integrity, and compassion, there is a better chance of developing an authentic duality.

4 **What advice can you give to the readers of this book to help them on their journeys with professional friends?**

Be your authentic self and give from the heart. Trust your instinct and be clear on your values. Be humble yet courageous. Once you have a professional friend, cultivate the relationship with care and with a commitment to respect their authentic self. Help them grow professionally and personally. Let them know that you are with them unconditionally. Be honest yet kind. Be motivating yet protective. Most of all, be just and always share your privilege to uplift the lives of friends. Friendships will not always be reciprocated, and that is when you must decide if the one-sided relationships are true professional friendships.

—Miriam Beloglovsky

Chapter Six

Circles of Friends

COMMUNITIES OF SUPPORT

Hello, Friend!

Early childhood education can be an isolating career choice. Educators often work in an environment filled with children but without other adults. The pandemic compounded this lonely existence by requiring even more social distance in our lives. We have collectively lived through challenging times. Besides your friends, what else did you turn to? Were you soothed by song? Music can bring solace when we are feeling stressed, isolated, and alone. Music can help us feel like we belong and that we have a wider community or circle of friends. It can help us feel less socially disconnected. A sense of belonging is one of the most basic and powerful human needs. It is a key to healthier and happier lives. When we sing and dance together, we create a sense of community as everyone moves together with shared intentions and a common goal.

As an exercise to consider the power of music in our professional lives, think about what would be on your friendship playlist. Do you have a favorite song about friendship? There are so many! Like a heartfelt quote, music has a way of saying things that are hard to express, and a song lyric can capture the way we feel. "With a Little Help from My Friends," written by the dynamic duo of John Lennon and Paul McCartney, is often stuck in my head. Are you hearing a friendship song in your head right now? Is it stuck there like an earworm? I try to embrace my earworms as they come and go by relating them to my professional friends. Songs bring my life comfort, and they feel like friends too. I get by with a little help from my friends, past, present, and future.

The Beatles are part of the soundtrack of my childhood. Going into my teenage years, it was Carole King and James Taylor who spoke to me through their music. "You've Got a Friend" from the album *Tapestry* will always remind me of Ann, a cherished forever friend. We met at camp, working as counselors, and she was my first professional friend. We helped each other navigate the social contexts of summer camp and being a teenager in the 1970s. We now have shared memories of these and many other experiences that have shaped our identities and friendship to this day.

This chapter is about how we can continue to make shared memories with our friends and to cultivate friendships that last throughout our lifespans. It is about keeping friends by growing rich and powerful relationships. By strengthening your friendships, you can build a legacy through which others can learn from you. This is your opportunity to give back. It is your opportunity to pass on the love and kindness that has characterized your friendships to others.

Building Friendships to Last a Lifetime

With a strong foundation, time, and effort, our professional friendships can endure. We will continue to reap the benefits of having friends as we grow old. When we honor our friendships with a loving commitment to the relationships, we are working to make sure they stand the test of time and the changing seasons. Author and family therapist Dr. Kathy McCoy (2022) suggests that being friends for life requires resilience, accepting change, being grateful, and focusing on commonalities rather than differences. Friends for life commit to closeness even when they are divided by miles. They are tolerant if there are time lapses in the relationship. McCoy suggests seven ways to build a friendship that can last a lifetime. I have added an eighth way:

1. Reciprocity. Kindnesses go both ways as needed.
2. Make room for growth and change. Be able to weather the changes of life.
3. Continually find connections. Go beyond what the initial attraction was and make sure to cultivate your common identity with many shared interests.
4. Give more weight to commonalities. Give less attention to your differences.

5. Commit to maintain the friendship across miles. Send a text, an email, or even a warm snail mail letter or card. Call or, even better, video chat so you can see the face of your friend. This is how you can stay connected if miles come between you and your friend.
6. Be tolerant of time lapses. If it seems like a long time since you have heard from a dear friend, understand that sometimes life gets busy. Show you care by staying in touch or keeping a respectful distance if that is what your friend needs.
7. Be open to new old friendships. A new old friend would be someone with whom you were once close but lost touch. Or it could be a past acquaintance who wasn't your friend then but could be now.
8. Play, laugh, dance, and sing together. Bring your friends together, take inspiration from children, and have fun.

Our professional friendships take effort, but they are worth it! Even when a friendship ends, there is always hope that the friend might in the future become a new old friendship. Do you share my wish that a friend or acquaintance from the past might become part of a friendship of the present and future? A friendship that has a foundation from the past and that is rekindled in the present can have a strong and solid future.

Cultivating Cultures of Friendship

> *Some people go to priests; others to poetry;*
> *I to my friends.*~ Virginia Woolf, *The Waves*

If you cultivate an attitude, image, or skill, you try hard to develop it and make it stronger. When we cultivate a friendship, we give it special attention. Within every learning environment, there is a prevailing culture that influences all the other components. Culture involves the dominant values and beliefs that influence decision-making within the environment. Contemplate the following three questions as you consider what it means to cultivate a culture of friendship:

1. What if friendships were encouraged among teachers and children?
2. What if there were a shared belief about the value of friendships?
3. What if we worked hard to develop a culture of friendship to make it stronger and better?

The Mud Kitchen as a Dyad Space
Photo Credit: Diane Kashin

Nancy Lauter (2004), an early childhood education scholar, offers the following suggestions for fostering friendships between children that might also cultivate a culture of friendship. After reading each bullet point, ask yourself what could happen if we applied this to professional adult relationships.

- Consider the environment. Work on establishing dyad spaces where two children can play in proximity.
- Provide materials that can be shared. Look for materials that are big and stationary and require more than one child to move. When two children work together, it is an opportunity for a friendship to form and strengthen.
- Encourage children to play in groups of two. When children are just beginning to learn social skills, it is difficult to deal with more than one peer at a time.
- Give children opportunities to play without direct adult supervision. Adults can take on a secondary role and encourage children to interact with a peer.
- Avoid interfering too quickly in a confrontation between peers. Children can collaboratively problem solve when they are given time and support.
- Avoid interjecting your values unless a child asks for your assistance. It may seem unfair to you if two children are playing and one child has 90

percent of the blocks. Pause and consider the complex social relationship at play. The children may not perceive this uneven distribution as negative. The children are growing in their understanding of their social world. Continue to observe to understand.

- Remember that onlookers learn by watching. Avoid insisting that onlookers join a group, recognizing that some children are not ready to be everyone's friend.
- Refrain from imposing friendships on children. Friendships need time to develop.

Friendships are important in the lives of children; it pays to foster these relationships when we can. We are learning about how the pandemic interrupted and changed children's friendships, and it confirms that children need friends. In a study conducted in 2020, participants ages five to fourteen were interviewed via a videoconferencing platform. The study revealed that children care deeply about their friends. The researchers found three central themes, and these are depicted in figure 6.1. For children, nothing replaces their friends. Children had virtual access to their friends during school closures, but it was not a substitute for being in the same space with their friends (Larivière-Bastien et al. 2022).

Children have always needed friends. This shared experience of the pandemic reinforced the significance of friendships in the lives of children. When we engage in a parallel process of reflection on the value of friendships, we can see that the benefits of friends extend to people of all ages. Early childhood educators can help develop a culture of friendship within their classrooms. Outside of the classroom, they can cultivate their own professional friendships. We need friends, now more than ever.

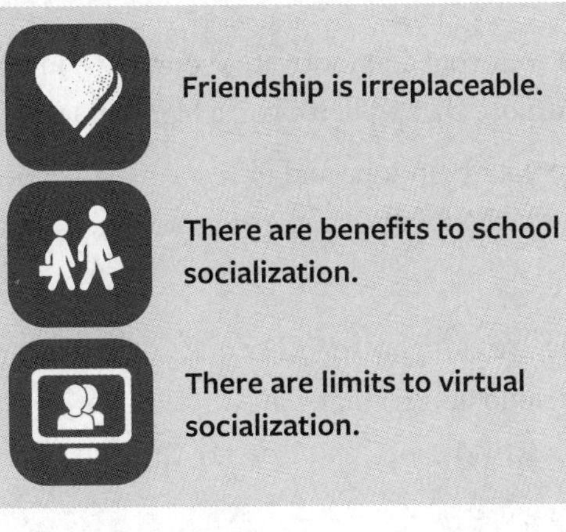

Figure 6.1 Themes of Friendship during the Pandemic

It is time to give ourselves permission to feel good again, and this involves reconnecting to what brings us joy. Robyne Hanley-Dafoe, a resiliency and wellness scholar and speaker, suggests that we look for ways to cultivate joy. What are the experiences that bring you hope-filled feelings and that leave you energized? Make a list of what brings you unique and blissful moments of joy. On top of my list are my professional friends!

Once you make a list of what brings you joy, Hanley-Dafoe (2022) suggests being intentionally aware of your joy and offers these eight strategies for strengthening the joyfulness. We can take the advice and implement it with professional friends.

1. Scheduling: Make time to play and create. Put aside time to be unproductive. Take time to feel your feelings.
2. Celebration: Recognize efforts and small and big wins. Celebrate little moments that could be victories on the rise. Celebrations are not just for the big moments; commemorate the small ones too.
3. Awareness and intention: Intentionally affirm your desire to bring to your life more joy, ease, creativity, and flow. Talk about your intentions with your friends to increase awareness.
4. Attitude: Create your reality by choosing a different perspective to see through. Embrace curiosity and lightheartedness enthusiastically.
5. Music: Create the soundtrack of a joyful life. Music has the power to uplift, boost, transform, and validate your moods. Enjoy the hunt for new songs that inspire and soothe to add to your mood playlist.
6. Follow the energy: When we feel good, it gives us more energy to do the things we love and to make an impact. Together with your friends, search out the people, experiences, and responsibilities that bring life and energy to your life.
7. Spirit and soul: What feeds your soul and motivates you to live in a way that feels good? Find the purpose that will give you a higher power.
8. Reclaim: You have a right to your emotions and to recovery. Take time to reclaim your emotions by being mindful and giving attention to your emotional state.

With our professional friends, we can play together and collectively contemplate big ideas, using our friendship to make an impact. Through our relationships, we can make the world a better place for the children and families we serve. By bringing friendship to the forefront and making it visible, we can cultivate a culture of friendship for all.

Making Friendship Visible

In early childhood education, we feel the inspiration of the Reggio Emilia approach when we speak of "making learning visible" through the process of pedagogical documentation. What might happen if we made friendship visible, bringing to life the important learning that comes from peer-to-peer relationships?

Offer children an opportunity to talk about their friends as a group or individually. Children can create drawings of their friends. They can write and illustrate books about their friendships. Communication boxes invite children to offer gifts and send messages to their friends. Observe children during make-believe play to learn more about their perspectives on friendship.

Imagine a learning environment where friendship is visible in this way. Together, teachers and children can explore a wider definition of friendship. They can realize that they have school friends, friends they grew up with, home friends, and grown-up friends. Children will see that they have more friends than perhaps they imagined. Having friends feels good to children. Learning to speak the language of friendship helps them keep their friendships strong and viable.

Griffen's Friends

Photo Credit: Diane Kashin

Griffen loves to draw. I can see that his drawings help him make sense of the world. During the pandemic, Griffen spent a considerable amount of time in virtual school. He missed seeing his friends in real time and would often draw pictures of them. Drawings help children express their thoughts and feelings in relation to particular events, such as friendships that were formed but interrupted.

Children want and need a way to express their thoughts and feelings about friendships. A study of kindergarten-age children in Canada found that young children really want to share their perspectives on their social lives and peer groups (Streelasky 2022). Children and teachers can become researchers undertaking a collaborative inquiry about friendships within a culture where friendship is cultivated. United Kingdom researchers Caron Carter and Cathy Nutbrown (2016) found that a group of children ages five and six were keen to draw and talk about their pictures because they were aware that their drawings were valued and appreciated. The emphasis was on what the children had to say about their drawings rather than the drawings per se.

In the same study, the researchers invited children to play with a set of miniature figures representing a small world. Small world play is an approach where children use figures and open-ended materials to create stories. The researchers provided a canvas for children to express their feelings about their friends in an imaginative and creative way. In addition to the materials, the children were asked a set of semi-structured questions about different friendship scenarios (Carter and Nutbrown 2016). Small world play revealed that children need their friends and that, during the process of the play, children could work through the complexities of relationships. In this world, children have control and power.

When children create miniature representations of their relationships, it helps them conceptually grasp the big picture. The creation of small worlds provides a concrete vehicle for understanding abstract ideas and complex feelings. David Sobel, who advances the philosophy of place-based education, writes that "small worlds work wonders for children. They provide the same kind of emotional security that islands provide for vacationers. The world is simplified and knowable" (Sobel 2008, 46). According to Sobel, small world play is cognitively accessible, meaning children and adults can grasp the different elements as they are brought together into a single view. Small world play can be an effective pedagogical tool for professional learning as well.

In Your Mind's Eye

Imagine you have been invited to create a small world at a workshop. You are presented with materials and invited to represent an environment that supports well-being and self-regulation. You have recently exchanged harsh words with one of your fellow teachers, and you wonder what they might be saying about you behind your back. You are thankful that you are not working in the same small group with that person, but just being in the same room is uncomfortable. The little peg people and other miniature loose parts and materials are a great distraction. At the end of the day, you reflect on this powerful small world professional learning experience. It made you think more deeply about how important friendships are in the lives of children. You are excited about supporting a culture of friendship but wish that you did not have the lingering sadness and anger from the confrontation that took place before the workshop. On the way home, you consider how bringing these feelings into your work environment may not be optimal for you, your colleagues, and the children. As you review the photos of the small world play, you realize that children and adults can take time to listen to their friends and to forgive when necessary. Children and adults need the skills of listening and forgiveness to maintain their friendships.

Small World Play

Photo Credit: Diane Kashin

As you examine notes, photos, and videos of children engaged in peer-to-peer relationships, how can you apply what you see in a parallel process of co-inquiry and investigation about professional friendships?

Making Connections to Pedagogical Practice: The Friendship Inquiry

When you observe children, is there evidence that they are interested in friendships? Most likely, you will see children in various stages of forming and maintaining friendships. A long-term friendship inquiry will support children's holistic development. It will also help you cultivate a culture of friendship, demonstrating to children that you value and appreciate their friendships and friendship struggles.

Provoking Proposal: Invite children to reflect and think deeply about friendships. Provide children with dyad spaces, books about friendships, and opportunities to create small worlds. Have materials available for children to represent friendships in drawings and stories. Interview every child throughout the friendship inquiry to document their theories and thoughts about friendships.

A friendship inquiry is an example of a collaborative play and learning experience for everyone! It can be a way to make friendship visible in a growing culture of friendship.

Calling a Circle of Friends

A professional friend can be a champion for life, someone who will advocate for your success. All you need is one other person to form a professional friendship. But what would happen if you had a group of friends? Would the benefits increase exponentially? I had an idea about calling a circle together. When a few of my dearest professional friends were planning a get-together, I knew that it was the perfect time to float my idea of forming a community of professional friends. In such a community, no single person in charge makes decisions about agendas and group dynamics. When we come together in a circle of support (CoS), we generate a common identity based on shared interests and joint activities. Learning with others who are professional friends is an experience of mutual affection. To learn and grow within a CoS is about friendships, voice, love, and kindness. It represents a common commitment to each other and shared ownership of the circle.

CoS members are always welcome, and attendance is never taken. The group meets virtually when face-to-face meetings are not possible. Combining online and in-person gatherings increases the group's accessibility, which is a boon because the circle aspires to be open. In the CoS that I gathered, members range in age, experience, and position held in the sector, though we are all early childhood educators from across Ontario. We represent different backgrounds, cultures, and perspectives. Every member is a leader in their context, and they work directly with children, teach or have taught early childhood education, or manage early childhood programs and agencies. Members include consultants and municipal early learning leaders. These are my relations, as my friend Hopi has said. Some are lifelong friends, and others are new friends.

A CoS is a community of practice (CoP) with a mission that focuses on hearing everyone's voice as a competent and capable professional friend. Members of a CoP share a common concern or passion for something they do, and by interacting regularly, they learn how to do it better. There are CoPs focused on infants and toddlers, preschoolers, kindergartners, and school-age children. Others share a commitment to specific domains of interests, such as risky play, loose parts, outdoor play, and so on. Ultimately, CoPs can engage with other CoPs for knowledge sharing and collective action. If you are aware of a CoP or are currently a member of a CoP, consider these five questions.

1. How is the domain of interest identified and by whom?
2. Who decides the boundaries of the interest?
3. Do all members of the community have similar values related to the interest?
4. Do all members have similar roles and opportunities to speak up in the CoP?
5. What activities do members engage in while pursuing the interest?

During the pandemic, I was asked to join a virtual CoP. Many of the decisions had been made prior to the meeting. I was not given an opportunity for input into the structure, logistics, protocols, or agenda setting of the CoP. The topic and direction came only from the organizers. The members were there to receive the information being delivered. I felt voiceless, and it felt more like being part of a focus group than a community. The tension created by feeling voiceless and powerless affected my experience. When bringing together a community, the goal should be to avoid a top-down experience where some members are not heard. According to the College of Early Childhood Educators (2018), engaging in a CoP supports reflective practices and collaborative inquiries. The voices and perspectives of all members should be reflected in the work of a CoP.

- *Community* means that members share experiences and build relationships in order to learn from and with each other.
- *Practice* means members from the community share a common practice. They develop a shared repertoire of experiences, stories, tools, guidelines, and procedures leading to a collective practice.
- *Knowledge domain* defines the community—the subject at hand.

These three factors continually influence each other. Experiences from the practice provide for shifts in the domain. These shifts in the domain have continued effects on the community.

In the book *Reflecting in Communities of Practice*, authors Deb Curtis, Debbie Lebo, Wendy C. M. Cividanes, and Margie Carter explain how one person in a CoP can serve the role of critical friend and take responsibility for provoking critical thinking in others: "A critical friend consciously works to bring out the knowledge of the participants or thoughtfully encourages members of the community to explore their knowledge of theory, research, and best practice in order to deepen the understanding of the topic at hand" (Curtis et al. 2013, 19). This role can be taken by a member of the CoP, or it can be a responsibility of the facilitator.

The main role of the facilitator is to help the group move forward with the mission of the CoP. As Curtis and coauthors explain, "Facilitators give individual attention to group members, monitor group dynamics, offer clarification on issues or confusions, point out breakthroughs in understanding, and periodically summarize the ideas generated" (Curtis et al. 2013, 18). While the facilitator tries not to dominate discussions or tell others what they need to know, their role still requires leadership and management skills and has responsibilities and decision-making power. The critical friend also has decision-making powers in their management of the dialogue and group dynamics. Both hold more powerful roles than other members. It takes a skilled facilitator and critical friend to ensure all voices are continually heard.

Would you be interested in joining a CoP with one facilitator and one critical friend? Or are you interested in a CoP that is a CoS? CoPs are not usually advertised. Finding one to join can require investigative work, initiative, and creativity. Early childhood educators have the competence and capacity to create their own learning communities to realize their professional hopes, dreams, and goals.

To start a CoS requires thought before action. First you must consider why you wish to initiate the group; what will your aims and goals be? Figure 6.2 offers a possible strategic direction.

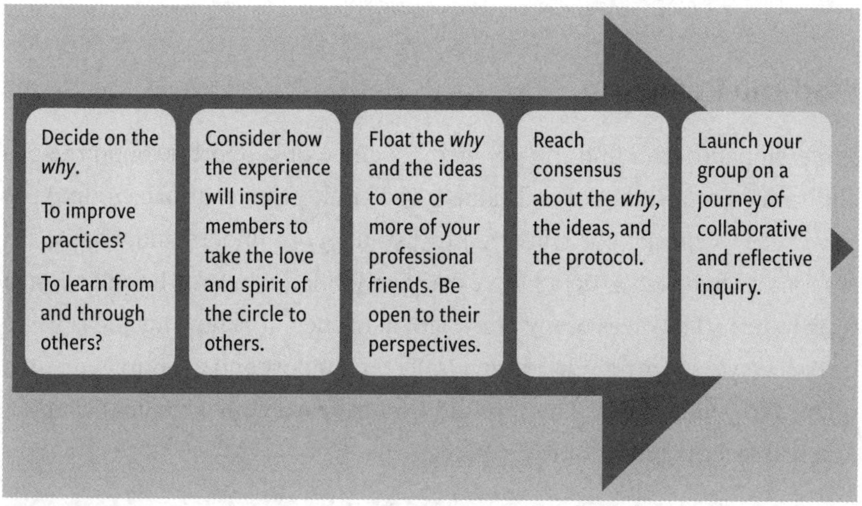

Figure 6.2 Steps to a CoS Launch

Germinating a CoP with others creates something that can be sustained across generations. A CoP can be a CoS when you set up a supportive community where there is transparency and agreement with the group's protocol, including the rules and procedures that govern it. Sharing is part of the Sacred Circles that I have experienced with Hopi. A protocol is followed wherein one eagle feather is passed around. With feather in hand, we share our identity with the rest of the circle.

For a CoP to become a CoS, members must dedicate time to learning about and from one another. It is through these relationships that we grow and improve. Learning about one another is as important or more important than discussing the topic at hand, because it creates a CoP experience where all voices are heard and individual identities are embraced.

Nidhi Menon considers perspectives of women of color to examine and deconstruct dominant narratives and structures of childhoods, suggesting that we can "reimagine traditional constructions of CoPs in order to redefine them as a space that amplifies the voices of ECEs to unsettle their continued marginalization through professional norms" (Menon 2022, 3). Drawing upon the work of Black feminist scholars, CoPs can be spaces to have crucial conversations about anti-racist pedagogy and make visible the participants' lived experiences. CoPs can be about creating space for painful but necessary discussions. CoPs should not be about reinforcing systems that continue to marginalize and render early childhood educators as voiceless.

Find the Power

Professional friends find their power in a circle of support. Around the circle, each voice is honored and valued. The circle gives you space to find the power (1) to speak your truth, (2) to listen, (3) to understand, and (4) to respond to support. I am a better early childhood educator because I take time to hear the voices of my professional friends. It is now my pleasure to introduce you to my circle of friends. Their support and encouragement is offered to you as a gift. They are the friends featured in this final chapter. You will feel the power of their words.

> *This is a place of comfort, calm, and listening. We can all feel safe and heard here.—Rosalba*

> *When you find a professional friend, it is a very humbling experience. Personally, my professional relationships evolved into personal relationships. Throughout my career, I now realize, I've spent more time in the midst of my professional relationships than I ever did with family or friends outside of work.—Cindy*

> *You know your friends are real when they stick. You may not always agree, or you may have a different outcome in mind, but those that stick with you are your true professional friends.—Stephanie*

> *When we are grappling with heavy issues, we need our friends to help us sort through it all. We can try to replicate ways to use our reflections on those experiences to make things better for children and families.—Amanda*

> *By being together, we are holding a space of kindness and respect for one another.—Sheryl*

I have leaned on my friends for balance and growth as an individual and professional. I have made some amazing professional friends who became dear friends outside of the workplace.—Nadine

In a small community, professional friends come and go as turnover is high. Now I have ones that stick because even though we are not all ECEs, we do similar work.—Jessica

When I think about my personal and professional relationships, there are no barriers, no walls between one or the other. They bring spirit and soul and light and becoming into my work and into my life.—Laura

My friends bring me back to myself as much as they connect me to the world beyond myself. That freedom and vulnerability in knowing that it is okay—and everyone agrees it is okay (if not better)—to go off script and off topic and let our minds, voices, and hearts wander in conversation, from whatever potentially proposed topic, is so important. There is a trust that whatever comes up and out will be magic.—Nicole

To care so much about our work and profession and share it with others, and for them to care so much too—that reciprocity feeds the soul. It fuels me to think that in our world with children, in the life we create together, we are creating a life we want to be in. We are our very best selves, and we see that in these friendships we share this world with. Thinking about how we need one another, we need to build our relationships as educators to find joy and support and, yes, to challenge one another, but I think we need a foundation together of trust, respect, and understanding. When you find someone that shares your excitement, they are like family with shared passion and love.—Tanya

The negative moments make us value the supportive friends who help us make sense of things. Professional friends remind us that we need to take care of ourselves and be true to our values and integrity. As givers by nature, we have to take care of ourselves and give ourselves the gifts of time, reflection, and perhaps even redirection or purpose.—Evette

A lot of my professional friendships evolve into personal friendships. In my role working with reconciliation, professional relationships are on a deeper level. This is because reconciliation is so important. A lot of times, we meet in passing, and you don't know when you are going to see each other again. If you stay connected, it can evolve into a beautiful friendship on a personal and professional level.—Melanie

When I used to think of mentors or those I admired as facilitators/speakers/teachers, I was intimidated and thought I needed to be more like them.

Now I walk alongside many of them, and I know it is about being myself on the journey.—Sheri

I think the depth of our relationships in ECE is so powerful that if some don't work out, the loss is also felt so deeply. It is a different kind of job than going to work in an office. Sometimes relationships become friendships that feel like family.—Paola

There will be some who are resistant to collaboration. When my input is dismissed as having no educational value, it is hard to be friends with that colleague.—Ruby

Whether it is a family circle, a circle of support, or a professional, personal, or social circle—we need those circles to be whole human beings. The answer to our challenges is to find that circle—even if it is only two or three friends who meet every so often, perhaps every moon cycle.—Hopi

When we gather together in our CoS, we are thinking about our core values and the things that really speak to our hearts, our hopes, and our dreams for ourselves, the children, and their families. These conversations keep going on in our heads, sustaining us as we nurture, support, and give back to others.

Big Ideas of Professional Friendships: Legacy and Giving Back

Being charitable is to give and to be benevolent, altruistic, helpful, accepting, and gracious. These prosocial behaviors help children and adults form and maintain friendships. Giving is a big idea. Giving back offers an opportunity to create generations layered by love and friendship. This can be your legacy. Imagine the possibilities that befriending your colleagues could make in your professional life. Imagine how this gift can keep on giving from one generation to the next.

You were asked at the beginning of this book what you would you pass on to the next generation of early childhood educators. Think of your legacy as a gift, an inheritance, or a bequest. Imagine passing on the gift of professional friendship. Imagine every early childhood educator working and growing alongside children within a culture of friendship. In the words of Hopi, "All life and learning must give back to the whole community to continue" (Martin 2021, 165).

Grand Bend Beachcombing with Amanda and Sheri

Photo Credit: Diane Kashin

Establishing traditions is one way to pass on gifts to the next generation. Journalist Gyan Yankovich (2022) suggests that we make and maintain friendships through traditions. While most families have formal and informal rituals, developing and celebrating traditions among friends comes with its own joy, especially when built on a shared interest. Can you gather a circle of professional friends who share an interest, while offering each other love and support?

1. Do you think gathering a CoS made up of professional friends is important to your development?
2. How often will you meet, and how long will your meeting be?
3. What will be the format of the gatherings: face-to-face, virtual, or a combination of both?
4. How would you begin your first gathering?
5. How will decisions be made about subsequent gatherings?
6. Are there any other traditions that your circle of friends can engage in together?
7. How can you sustain your circle of friends and ensure that participants feel comfortable to share their voices?
8. What advice would you give others if they are interested in calling a circle together?

Thinking Back

My former friend introduced me to a beachcombing tradition that continues to be an important part of my life and friendships. I vividly remember walking and talking together while looking for stones that told stories and beach glass treasures that sparkled in the sun. Now my favorite time to reflect and connect is while strolling any beach, but particularly the shores of Lake Huron in a little beach town called Grand Bend, a place of glorious sunrises and sunsets. I often think about my former friend when I am on the beach stooping over to pick up a glistening piece of glass. I remember our many conversations and musings about pedagogy and practice. I continue to be fascinated with beach glass and wonder about the origin of each piece. How long was the shard of colorful glass tumbled by the waves, sand, and stone? Legend has it that pieces of beach glass are really the tears of a mermaid banned to the bottom of the water because of her love for a sea captain. Her tears arrive on the shore as beautifully colored glass, a symbol of love. I will always be grateful for this introduction to beachcombing and will carry on the tradition with family and friends. When I collect beach glass, I can tearfully recall friendships that have ended, but I find comfort in the gifts of time that the act of beachcombing represents. It is a gift to have these moments to be with friends while engaged in a shared experience bonded by a common interest. The beach glass is a symbol of love among friends.

Thank You for Being a Friend

Beach glass has become a symbol of my professional friendships. I also like to contemplate other symbols of friendship. The infinity symbol is the coming together of two circles, representing the concept of limitlessness or eternity. As a symbol of friendship, infinity suggests the absence of the beginning and the end. It demonstrates the eternal connection between the love of friends.

We can show gratitude to our professional friends with the gift of a friendship symbol such as a friendship bracelet. In this tradition, you make a wish when the bracelet is tied on, and if the bracelet falls off naturally because the threads have worn through, the wish will come true! On the other hand, it is bad luck to remove a friendship bracelet, as this might represent that the friendship has cooled.

Rose quartz is the stone of unconditional love, and the deep-blue lapis lazuli is a symbol of friendship and of truth. A strong, long-lasting friendship is the most honest. We rely on our friends to tell us the truth when nobody else can or will. Friends who stand by us through thick and thin, and always tell it like it is, are our true friends. The carnelian gemstone is considered a spiritual symbol of friendship. It evokes fire, but it's also a breath of fresh air. Carnelian sparks creativity and empowers your inner voice. Carnelian instills self-esteem as well as feelings of fraternity with your friends. With bonus attributes such as sociability, emotional warmth, and awareness of the feelings of others, carnelian is a powerful all-around gemstone for friendship. The amethyst helps with communication, balance, and stress while guiding positive transformation. The Hebrew word for amethyst, *ahlamah*, translates to "dream stone." This purple beauty encourages dreams for the next generation.

Symbols of friendship can become treasures that represent the stories of your professional friendships over the seasons of your life. It is my hope that the concept of professional friends will inspire many stories within stories. You will have stories to tell when you move in relationship with professional friends. Your friends will have stories to share too.

My final story takes place around a sacred fire with Hopi. There I sat with new and old friends in a spirit of love and affection as we remembered others who could not be there. When the feather passed to me, I shared a piece of my heart while feeling the strength of my ancestors. As I spoke about Bubbie Dorothy, Grandma Molly, and the beautiful Dina, three crows perched on a tall tree, looking toward me. I felt immense gratitude to my ancestors and my professional friends. When I stood up to put tobacco on the fire, the crows flew away. I waved goodbye to my grandmothers and felt their strength and love.

My dear friend Nicole eloquently and tearfully talked about how our friends help us be who we really are. Our friends bring us home to ourselves. This is how learning happens. This is how we make meaning of our lives. By cultivating professional friendships, you are building a circle of support. By supporting and encouraging friendships across the early learning ecosystem, you will be part of a world of love and kindness. Thank you, my friends, for helping make meaning of my life's work and passion. Thank you for all the gifts I have received from each and every one of you. It is through you that I have arrived home to myself. May the words of my circle of friends inspire you to explore the role of friendships in your own unique and beautiful contexts.

Four Questions for My Circle of Friends

1. **After reading the chapter, what sparked your interest?**

   Professional friends are an antidote to loneliness. You can have sincere warm feelings for colleagues, but when you have a professional friend, it is much deeper, and the care is greater. To be a friend is to take the time to listen. You can't be friends with everyone, but you can always listen, which will sometimes lead to deep and meaningful relationships. It takes time to have a professional friendship. Children need time to build relationships and work through problems and conflicts. We are in a parallel process of forging and maintaining friendships alongside children!

2. **As you considered this spark/interest, how has your thinking moved with it?**

   Stretch time to build on existing professional friendships. Slow down to forge new connections and cultivate old friends. This is time well spent as these friends will be invaluable to your professional growth and success. Move with your friends, play, and laugh together while thinking deeply about what is possible for children and families within a culture of friendship.

3. **After considering questions one and two, what connections are you making to your own experiences with professional friends?**

   Be with your professional friends without an agenda. Without asking anything from them, check in to see how they are. When people confide in you, they are probably not seeking advice unless they ask. They just want to be heard and sense your empathy. Be the listener, be the helper, but remember it is important for you to be heard and helped too. Professional friends will push you to think deeper, to reflect, and to grow. They will love and care for you when you need a friend.

4. **What advice can you give to the readers of this book to help them on their journeys with professional friends?**

   Just as you would with young children, practice the pedagogy of listening. Listen not to respond but to understand. We all need to feel respected and heard. Establish rituals and celebrate or acknowledge life's moments with your friends. Let them know they matter. Disagreements may happen, but remember to always be respectful and open. To learn from your professional friends requires you to first be truthful to yourself. This too may take time. It may take continuous effort to learn, question, think, and offer to others. If we stop questioning or listening, we have stopped living. A friendship is delicate but strong, and it takes commitment and work. The result is joyful pleasure that makes us feel good emotionally, cognitively, and physically. Humans need other humans; we need kindness, care, and friendship. We can't be islands. We need professional friends in our workplaces, and in our lives as a whole. If you are forging a new friendship, start with someone you feel safe and comfortable with, and be open and honest. Set limitations and boundaries. It is hard to be supportive when your cup is empty. When your cup is full, you will see that it can spill over with all the love and kindness that you have experienced, causing a ripple effect that creates circles of friends within circles of friends. Your friends will help you find your *why*, your purpose in life. This will be your friendship legacy.

References

Introduction

Allen, S. 2018. *The Science of Gratitude*. West Conshohocken, PA: John Templeton Foundation.

Baskerville, D., and H. Goldblatt. 2009. "Learning to Be a Critical Friend: From Professional Indifference through Challenge to Unguarded Conversations." *Cambridge Journal of Education* 39 (2): 205–21.

Costa, A. L., and B. Kallick. 1993. "Through the Lens of a Critical Friend." *Educational Leadership* 51 (2): 49–51.

Edwards, C. P. 2004. "Thinking about Friendships: Fostering and Extending Young Children's Understanding." In *Connecting: Friendship in the Lives of Young Children*, edited by B. Neugebauer and D. P. Wolf, 28–33. Lincoln, NE: Exchange Press.

Elkind, D. 2015. *Giants in the Nursery: A Biographical History of Developmentally Appropriate Practice*. St. Paul, MN: Redleaf Press.

Emmons, R. A., J. Froh, and R. Rose. 2019. "Gratitude." In *Positive Psychological Assessment: A Handbook of Models and Measures*, edited by M. W. Gallagher and S. J. Lopez, 317–32. Washington, DC: American Psychological Association.

Gandini, L. 2011. "Play and the Hundred Languages of Children: An Interview with Lella Gandini." *American Journal of Play* 4 (1): 1–18.

Goldberg, E. 2022. "The Magic of Your First Work Friends." *New York Times*, July 14, 2022.

Kimmerer, R. W. 2013. *Braiding Sweetgrass: Indigenous Wisdom, Scientific Knowledge and the Teachings of Plants*. Minneapolis, MN: Milkweed Editions.

Martin, H. 2021. "Listening to Land as Teacher in Early Childhood Education." PhD diss., University of Toronto.

Murphy, K. 2020. *You're Not Listening: What You Are Missing and Why It Matters*. New York: Celadon Books.

Nell, M., W. F. Drew, and D. E. Bush. 2013. *From Play to Practice: Connecting Teachers' Play to Children's Learning*. Washington, DC: National Association for the Education of Young Children.

Ontario Ministry of Education. 2014. *How Does Learning Happen? Ontario's Pedagogy for the Early Years*. Toronto: Ontario Ministry of Education.

Page, J. 2018. "Characterising the Principles of Professional Love in Early Childhood Care and Education." *International Journal of Early Years Education* 26 (2): 125–41.

Parlakian, R., and S. B. Hoffman. 2020. "Nurturing Gratitude." Zero to Three. Published November 18, 2020. www.zerotothree.org/resource/nurturing-gratitude.

Vygotsky, L. S. 1981. "The Genesis of Higher Mental Functions." In *The Concept of Activity in Soviet Psychology*, edited by J. V. Wertsch, 144–88. Armonk, NY: M. E. Sharpe.

Willems, M. 2007. *Knuffle Bunny Too*. New York: Hyperion Books.

Chapter One

Brewer, C. A., T. Wideman-Johnston, and M. McCabe. 2021. "Better Together: The Role of Critical Friendship in Empowering Emerging Academics." *In Education* 26 (2): 75–91.

Brown, B. 2021. *Dare to Lead*: The Braving Inventory. https://brenebrown.com/resources/the-braving-inventory/.

Degges-White, S. 2018. "Friendology: The Science of Friendship." *Psychology Today*, May 29, 2018. www.psychologytoday.com/ca/blog/lifetime-connections/201805/friendology-the-science-friendship.

Dietze, B., and D. Kashin. 2021. *Playing and Learning in Early Childhood Education.* 2nd ed. North York, ON: Pearson Canada.

Hawkins, D. 1974. "I, Thou, and It." In *The Informed Vision: Essays on Learning and Human Nature* by D. Hawkins, 48–62. New York: Agathon Publishing.

Jablon, J., N. Parks, and L. Ensler. 2021. *The Five Commitments of Optimistic Leaders for Children: A Reflective Practice Journal.* South Orange, NJ: Leading for Children.

Miller, J. 2014. "The Effectiveness of the Critical Friends Model for Teacher Collaboration." Master's thesis, California State University. https://digitalcommons.csumb.edu/caps_thes/587.

Paulus, M., N. Christner, and M. Wörle. 2020. "The Normative Status of Friendship: Do Young Children Enforce Sharing with Friends and Appreciate Reasonable Partiality?" *Journal of Experimental Child Psychology* 194 (June).

Reschke, K. 2019. "Who Am I? Developing a Sense of Self and Belonging." *Zero to Three* 39 (3): 5–8.

Rouse, E. 2012. "Partnerships in Early Childhood Education and Care: Empowering Parents or Empowering Practitioners." *Global Studies of Childhood* 2 (1): 14–25.

Schön, D. A. 1987. *Educating the Reflective Practitioner: Toward a New Design for Teaching and Learning in the Professions*. San Francisco: Jossey-Bass.

Chapter Two

Ferry, B. 2015. *Stick and Stone.* New York: Houghton Mifflin Harcourt.

———. 2021. *Stick and Stone: Best Friends Forever!* New York: Clarion Books.

Goleman, D. 1995. *Emotional Intelligence.* New York: Bantam Books.

Goleman, D., and R. Boyatzis. 2017. "Emotional Intelligence Has 12 Elements: Which Do You Need to Work On?" *Harvard Business Review* 84 (2): 1–5.

Housman, D. 2022. "Even Superheroes Need Support: Emotional Intelligence for Early Childhood Educators." *Exchange Magazine*, January/February.

Kline, N. 2020. "Let Me Finish: How to Stop Interrupting . . . and Change the World." *Guardian*, October 24, 2020. www.theguardian.com/lifeandstyle/2020/oct/24/let-me-finish-how-to-stop-interrupting-and-change-the-world.

Kolowich Cox. L. 2020. "Nine Ways to Deal with Imposter Syndrome before It Hinders Your Success." *Hubspot*, July 28, 2020. https://blog.hubspot.com/marketing/impostor-syndrome-tips.

Malaguzzi, L. 1993. "For an Education Based on Relationships." Translated by Lella Gandini. *Young Children* 49 (1): 9–12.

Murphy, K. 2020. *You're Not Listening: What You Are Missing and Why It Matters*. New York: Celadon Books.

———. 2021. "How to Rearrange Your Post-pandemic 'Friendscape.'" *New York Times*, June 7, 2021. www.nytimes.com/2021/06/01/well/family/curate-friends.html.

Noll, M. 2019. "Here's How Understanding the 5 Love Languages Strengthened My Friendship." *Yahoo*, December 18, 2019. www.yahoo.com/video/understanding-5-love-languages-strengthened-163058437.html.

Penfold, L. 2019. "Material Matters in Children's Creative Learning." *Journal of Design and Science*, February 19, 2019. https://jods.mitpress.mit.edu/pub/bwp6cysy.

Rinaldi, C. 2021. *In Dialogue with Reggio Emilia: Listening, Researching and Learning*. New York: Routledge.

Schulze, B. 2021. "Beth Ferry Discusses *Stick and Stone: Best Friends Forever!*" *The Children's Book Review*, September 2021. www.thechildrensbookreview.com/2021/09/beth-ferry-discusses-stick-and-stone-best-friends-forever.

Seneca, L. A. 1807. *Seneca's Morals by Way of Abstract: To Which Is Added, a Discourse, Under the Title of an After-thought*, edited by R. L'Estrange. London: Jacob Tonson.

Thoreau, H. D. 1906. *A Week on the Concord and Merrimack Rivers*. New York: Houghton Mifflin Company.

Tominey, S. L., E. C. O'Bryon, S. E. Rivers, and S. Shapses. 2017. "Teaching Emotional Intelligence in Early Childhood." *Young Children* 72 (1): 6–14.

Valle, Ron. 2019. "Toward a Psychology of Silence." *The Humanistic Psychologist* 47 (3): 219–61.

Vecchi, V. 2010. *Art and Creativity in Reggio Emilia: Exploring the Role and Potential of Ateliers in Early Childhood Education*. New York: Routledge.

Zangara, N. 2012. *Surviving Female Friendships: The Good, the Bad and the Ugly*. Chandler, AZ: Brighton Publishing.

Chapter Three

Bahns, A. J. 2019. "Preference, Opportunity, and Choice: A Multilevel Analysis of Diverse Friendship Formation." *Group Processes & Intergroup Relations* 22 (2): 233–52. https://doi.org/10.1177/1368430217725390.

Bertrand, J. 2017. The *Power of Friendship in Early Childhood Education.* Storypark video. Posted September 14, 2017. https://blog.storypark.com/2017/09/power-friendships-early-childhood-video.

Council of Australian Governments. 2009. *Belonging, Being, and Becoming: The Early Years Learning Framework for Australia.* Council of Australian Governments

Ferry, B. 2019. *The Scarecrow.* New York: HarperCollins.

Fraser, Susan. 2000. *Authentic Childhood: Experiencing Reggio Emilia in the Classroom.* Scarborough, ON: Nelson.

Hall, J. A. 2019. "How Many Hours Does It Take to Make a Friend?" *Journal of Social and Personal Relationships* 36, no. 4, 1278–1296.

Hedrik, M. 2015. "How Our Names Shape Our Identity." *The Week*, January 8, 2015. https://theweek.com/articles/460056/how-names-shape-identity.

Lipmanowicz, H., and K. McCandless. 2013. *The Surprising Power of Liberating Structures: Simple Rules to Unleash a Culture of Innovation.* Seattle, WA: Liberating Structures Press.

Lucas, F. 2019. "Spirituality Is an Aspect of Children's Self-Identity—but How Do We Teach It?" *The Sector*, April 15, 2019. https://thesector.com.au/2019/04/15/spirituality-is-an-aspect-of-childrens-self-identity-but-how-do-we-teach-it.

Martin, H. 2021. "Listening to Land as Teacher in Early Childhood Education." PhD diss., University of Toronto.

———. n.d. "Asemaa Nitam (Sacred Tobacco First)." Edge of the Bush. Accessed March 12, 2023. https://edgeofthebush.ca/asemaa-ntam-tobacco-first-protocol.

Max, J. 2007. *Spider Spins a Story: Fourteen Legends from Native America.* Flagstaff, AZ: Rising Moon Books.

Miller, P. 2022. *True Friends.* St. Lucia: University of Queensland Press.

Pathman, T., and P. J. Bauer. 2020. "Memory and Early Brain Development." In *Encyclopedia on Early Childhood Development* (online), edited by R. E Tremblay, M. Boivin, and R. Peters. Published June 2020. www.child-encyclopedia.com/brain/according-experts/memory-and-early-brain-development.

Razzetti, G. 2019. "What Are Liberating Structures and How Can They Facilitate Change." *Fearless Culture*, November 13, 2019. www.fearlessculture.design/blog-posts/what-are-liberating-structures-how-can-they-facilitate-change.

Rolfe, G., D. Freshwater, and M. Jasper. 2001. *Critical Reflection for Nursing and the Helping Professions: A User's Guide.* London: Palgrave.

Schein, D. 2017. *Inspiring Wonder, Awe, and Empathy: Spiritual Development in Young Children.* St. Paul, MN: Redleaf Press.

Schein, J., and D. Schein. n.d. *The Hundred Languages of Children Meet the 70 Faces of Torah.* New York: Jewish Education Project.

Seidman, G. 2018. "Why Do We Like People Who Are Similar to Us?" *Psychology Today,* December 18, 2018. www.psychologytoday.com/us/blog/close-encounters/201812/why-do-we-people-who-are-similar-us.

Stevenson, J. 1999. "The Circle of Healing." *Native Social Work Journal* 2 (1): 8–12.

TRC (Truth and Reconciliation Commission) of Canada. 2015. *Honouring the Truth, Reconciling for the Future: Summary of the Final Report of the TRC of*

Canada. Ottawa: TRC of Canada. https://publications.gc.ca/site/eng/9.800288/publication.html.
Wolf, D. 2004. "Friendship: More Than Social Skills." In *Connecting: Friendship in the Lives of Young Children*, edited by B. Neugebauer and D. P. Wolf. Lincoln, NE: Exchange Press.

Chapter Four

Axelsson, S. 2014a. "Bubble Game." *Interaction Imagination*, October 25, 2014. https://interactionimagination.blogspot.com/2014/10/bubble-game.html.
———. 2014b. "The Importance of the Spoken Language." *Interaction Imagination*, September 9, 2014. https://interactionimagination.blogspot.com/2014/09/the-importance-of-spoken-language.html.
———. 2022. *The Original Learning Approach*. St. Paul, MN: Redleaf Press.
Degges-White, S. 2018. "Friendology: The Science of Friendship." *Psychology Today*, May 29, 2018. www.psychologytoday.com/ca/blog/lifetime-connections/201805/friendology-the-science-friendship.
Dellitt, J. 2022. "8 Signs You're Outgrowing a Friendship—and What to Do about It." *Everygirl*, May 7, 2022. https://theeverygirl.com/9-signs-youre-outgrowing-a-friendship-and-what-to-do-about-it.
DeMarco, J. 2019. "How to Have a Healthy Friendship with Someone You Are Competing With." *Everygirl*, May 8, 2019. https://theeverygirl.com/how-to-have-a-healthy-friendship-with-someone-youre-competing-with.
Gilmour, P. 2021. "Jealous of Friends? Here Is How to Deal." *Cosmopolitan*, July 13, 2021. www.cosmopolitan.com/uk/love-sex/relationships/a37008192/jealous-of-friends/#:~:text=Jealousy%20in%20a%20relationship%20or,we%20feel%20jealous%20are%20counterproductive.
Gray, P. 2022. "What Is Play: How Children Define It." *Psychology Today*, May 15, 2022. www.psychologytoday.com/ca/blog/freedom-learn/202205/what-is-play-how-children-define-it.
Hawkins, D. 2002. *The Informed Vision: Essays on Learning and Human Nature*. New York: Algora Publishing.
Housman Institute. 2020. "Self-Care for Educators Should Be a Priority Now." Houseman Institute. Published September 30, 2020. www.housmaninstitute.com/blog/self-care-for-educators-make-it-a-priority-now.
Hoyos-Valdés, D. 2017. "The Notion of Character Friendship and the Cultivation of Virtue." *Journal for the Theory of Social Behaviour* 48 (1): 66–82.
Hussong, A. 2017. "What Parents Neglect to Teach about Gratitude." *Greater Good Magazine*, November 21, 2017. https://greatergood.berkeley.edu/article/item/what_parents_neglect_to_teach_about_gratitude.
Joseph, M., and C. Ravesi-Weinstein. 2020. "Educators Supporting Educators: You Can't Pour from an Empty Cup." Massachusetts Association for Supervision and Curriculum Development. Published July 20, 2020. www.mascd.org/blog/educators-supporting-educators-you-cant-pour-from-an-empty-cup-self-care-webinar.

Kashin, D. 1996. "Connecting Circles: Reflective Early Childhood Education Practice." Unpublished master's thesis, Ontario Institute for Studies in Education.

Kohler-Evans, P. 2022. "You Can't Pour from an Empty Cup: Nurturing Ourselves to Support Our Students." *Faculty Focus*, April 20, 2022. www.facultyfocus.com/articles/philosophy-of-teaching/you-cant-pour-from-an-empty-cup-nurturing-ourselves-to-support-our-students.

Lewis, C. S. 1960. *The Four Loves*. London: Geoffrey Bles.

Mata-McMahon, J., M. J. Haslip, and D. L. Schein. 2020. "Connections, Virtues, and Meaning-Making: How Early Childhood Educators Describe Children's Spirituality." *Early Childhood Education Journal* 48 (5): 657-69.

Miyakoshi, A. 2015. *Tea Party in the Woods*. Toronto: Kids Can Press.

Morin, A. 2020. "How to Teach Children Gratitude: It's More Than Just Saying Thank You." *Verywell Mind*, November 11, 2020. www.verywellmind.com/how-to-teach-children-gratitude-4782154.

Petticrew, G. 2018. "What Is True Friendship? What the Stoics Believed and How I Intend to Apply It." *Medium*, September 29, 2018. https://medium.com/wisehealthywealthy/what-is-true-friendship-1d027a543dcb.

Pinchover, S. 2017. "The Relation between Teachers' and Children's Playfulness: A Pilot Study." *Frontiers in Psychology* 8, art. 2214.

Popescu, A. 2019. "Why People Ghost and How to Get Over It." *New York Times*, January 22, 2019. www.nytimes.com/2019/01/22/smarter-living/why-people-ghost-and-how-to-get-over-it.html.

Vanbuskirk, S. 2021. "How to Help Your Child Handle a Fight with Friends." *Verywell Family*, November 5, 2021. www.verywellfamily.com/how-to-help-your-child-handle-a-fight-with-friends-5198377.

Wallin, K. 2003 *Pedagogical Somersaults: A Book about Swedish Children and the Inspiration from Reggio Emilia*. Stockholm: HLS Förlag.

Zosh, J. N., E. J. Hopkins, H. Jensen, C. Liu, D. Neale, K. Hirsh-Pasek, S. Lynneth Solis, and D. Whitebread. 2017. *Learning through Play: A Review of the Evidence*. Billund, Denmark: LEGO Foundation.

Chapter Five

Beloglovsky, M. 2022. *Just Play: Inspiring Adult Play in Early Childhood Education*. St. Paul, MN: Redleaf Press.

Brewer, C. A., T. Wideman-Johnston, and M. McCabe. 2021. "Better Together: The Role of Critical Friendship in Empowering Emerging Academics." *In Education* 26 (2): 75–91.

Burman, L. 2023. *A Culture of Agency: Fostering Engagement, Empowerment, Identity, and Belonging in the Early Years*. St. Paul, MN: Redleaf Press.

Carlsen, K., and A. Clark. 2022. "Potentialities of Pedagogical Documentation as an Intertwined Research Process with Children and Teachers in Slow Pedagogies." *European Early Childhood Education Research Journal* 30 (2): 200–212.

Carter, M. 2006. "Rethinking Conference Learning." *Exchange Magazine*, March/April. www.exchangepress.com/article/rethinking-conference-learning/5016824.

Carter, M., and D. Curtis. 2002. *Training Teachers: A Harvest of Theory and Practice.* St. Paul, MN: Redleaf Press.

———. 2012. *The Art of Awareness.* St. Paul, MN: Redleaf Press.

College of Early Childhood Educators. 2017. *Reflective Practice and Self-Directed Learning.* Toronto: College of Early Childhood Educators. www.college-ece.ca/en/Documents/CPL_Reflective_Practice_Self_Directed_Learning.pdf.

Csikszentmihalyi, M. 1997. *Finding Flow: The Psychology of Engagement with Everyday Life*. New York: Basic Books.

Daly, L., and M. Beloglovsky. 2015. "Introducing Loose Parts to Preschoolers." *Teaching Young Children* 9 (1): 18–20.

Draguicevich, T. 2021. "But Can I Trust You? Embracing Different Perspectives in an Early Childhood Classroom." *Young Children* 76 (4): 6269.

Edwards, C., L. Gandini, and G. Forman, eds. 1998. *The Hundred Languages of Children: The Reggio Emilia Approach to Early Childhood Education: Advanced Reflections.* Westport, CT: Ablex.

Elkind, D. 2001. *The Hurried Child: Growing Up Too Fast Too Soon.* 3rd ed. Cambridge, MA: Perseus Publishing.

Fleet, A., and C. Patterson. 2001. "Professional Growth Reconceptualized: Early Childhood Staff Searching for Meaning." In *Early Childhood Research and Practice* 3 (2): 1–15.

Galinsky, E. 2010. *Mind in the Making.* Washington, DC: National Association for the Education of Young Children.

Gray, P. 2016. "Biological Foundations for Self-Directed Education." *Psychology Today*, September 28, 2016. www.psychologytoday.com/ca/blog/freedom-learn/201609/biological-foundations-self-directed-education?eml.

Kashin, D. 2018. "Loose Parts: Children as Creators Rather Than Consumers." *Technology Rich Inquiry Based Research*, November 22, 2018. https://tecribresearch.blog/2018/11/22/loose-parts-children-as-creators-rather-than-consumers.

Martin, H. 2021. "Listening to Land as Teacher in Early Childhood Education." PhD diss., University of Toronto.

McLerran, A. 1991. *Roxaboxen.* New York: HarperCollins.

Neff, Kristin. 2019. *The Yin and Yang of Self-Compassion: Cultivating Kindness and Strength in the Face of Difficulty.* Louisville, CO: Sounds True.

Nicholson, S. 1971. "How NOT to Cheat Children: The Theory of Loose Parts." *Landscape Architecture* 62 (1): 30–34.

O'Brien, A. 2016. "Five Ways to Increase Teacher Agency in Professional Development." *Edutopia*, July 5, 2016. www.edutopia.org/blog/five-ways-increase-teacher-agency-professional-development-anne-obrien.

Chapter Six

Carter, C., and C. Nutbrown. 2016. "A Pedagogy of Friendship: Young Children's Friendships and How Schools Can Support Them." *International Journal of Early Years Education* 24 (4): 395-413.

College of Early Childhood Educators. 2018. *CPL Resource: Communities of Practice*. Toronto: College of Early Childhood Educators. www.college-ece.ca/en/Documents/CPL%20Resource-Communities-Of-Practice.pdf.

Curtis, D., D. Lebo, W. C. M. Cividanes, and M. Carter. 2013. *Reflecting in Communities of Practice: A Workbook for Early Childhood Educators*. St. Paul, MN: Redleaf Press.

Hanley-Dafoe, R. 2022. "Cultivating Joy after Change and Uncertainty." *Psychology Today*, July 19, 2022. www.psychologytoday.com/us/blog/everyday-resilience/202207/cultivating-joy-after-change-and-uncertainty?eml.

Larivière-Bastien, D., O. Aubuchon, A. Blondin, D. Dupont, J. Libenstein, F. Séguin, A. Tremblay, H. Zarglayoun, C. M. Herba, and M. H. Beauchamp. 2022. "Children's Perspectives on Friendships and Socialization during the COVID-19 Pandemic: A Qualitative Approach." *Child Care, Health, and Development* 48 (6): 1017–30.

Lauter, N. 2004. "Supporting Social Interaction between Toddlers." In *Connecting: Friendship in the Lives of Young Children and Their Teachers*, edited by B. Neugebauer and D. P. Wolf, 14–18. Lincoln, NE: Exchange Press.

Martin, H. 2021. "Listening to Land as Teacher in Early Childhood Education." PhD diss., University of Toronto.

McCoy, K. 2022. "7 Tips for Building Friendships to Last a Lifetime." *Psychology Today*, November 8, 2022. www.psychologytoday.com/ca/blog/complicated-love/202211/7-tips-building-friendships-last-lifetime.

Menon, N. 2022. "Reimagining Communities of Practice: Using Marginalized Feminist Knowledge to Create Spaces of Resistance." *eceLINK* 6 (1): 31–41.

Sobel, D. 2008. *Childhood and Nature: Design Principles for Educators*. Portsmouth, NH: Stenhouse Publishers.

Streelasky, J. 2022. "Kindergarten Children's Views on Friendship in a Super-Diverse Context." *Childhood* 29 (1): 94–111.

Woolf, V. (1931) 1992. *The Waves*. London: Oxford University Press.

Yankovich, G. 2022. "'We Don't Want It to Ever Stop': How to Make and Maintain a Friendship tradition." *Guardian*, July 16, 2022. www.theguardian.com/lifeandstyle/2022/jul/16/we-dont-want-it-to-ever-stop-how-to-make-and-maintain-a-friendship-tradition.